Dedication

To my loving wife, Dr. Marie Menna Pagliaro, whose patience and support have been the source of my strength and direction.

Everything You Should Know

ABOUT MUSICAL INSTRUMENTS

But Didn't Have Time to Learn

by Michael J. Pagliaro, Ph.D., Sc.D.

Published by
Columbia Pacific University Press
San Rafael, California

Distributed by
Ardsley Musical Instrument Services, Ltd.
Scarsdale, New York
1-800-VIBRATO

Published by
Columbia Pacific University Press
of
Columbia Pacific University
1415 Third Street, San Rafael, California 94901
Telephone: 415-459-1650

Reproductions in this book that are taken from other publications have been used with the permission of the respective publishers. The author expresses his special appreciation to Dr. Richard Crews, friend and mentor, whose technological expertise turned a concept for this book into a reality, and to Mr. Gregory Raciti for contributing his artistic talent and creativity in drawing the diagrams contained in this publication.

ISBN 0-945-86449-3

CONTENTS

PREFACE

The aim of this book is to facilitate the understanding of the design, construction, and acoustical systems of woodwind, brass, and non-fretted string instruments. The author presents some basic information on the fundamentals of the physics of sound along with a small glossary of terms and then discusses each instrument in detail.

The science of musical instruments is very complex and there is a tendency for music scholars to be rather verbose. The author has tried to offer simple presentations on how musical instruments work. He has added illustrations and appendices to help further understanding without the need for extensive, long-winded readings. The information he has supplied should increase the understanding of how musical instruments work, while allowing the reader to apply this knowledge to any chosen field of specialization.

The format of the text makes it easy either to read the manual from cover to cover or to find a fact relevant to a particular instrument. All chapters are short and to the point. Any term introduced for the first time is italicized. Diagrams showing the parts of the instruments under discussion are presented whenever applicable. This format speeds up the search for information and is 'reader friendly'.

CHAPTER ONE

THE SCIENCE OF SOUND

Sound occurs when a force excites vibrations in the atmosphere. These vibrations are projected by a series of compressed and released waves of air pressure. Molecules of air are pushed against each other acting like a train would when the last car is pushed and each car preceding the last one responds in turn in a chain reaction. Since one single molecule of air cannot travel very far on its own, the molecules must push against each other in order to permit the sound to travel.

When this action and reaction take place in the air, a wavelike motion produces groupings of molecules positioned in alternating sequences. The first grouping of compressed molecules is referred to as *compression*. The grouping created by the void left behind the compression is in a more open spacial relationship and is called *rarefaction*. It is the combined action of compression and rarefaction that results in one complete cycle (fig. 1.1).

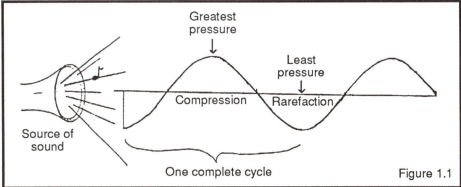

Figure 1.1

When vibration is initiated on a string, movement begins at the point of rest or equilibrium (fig. 1.2, point A). The movement proceeds to its upper limit (point B), then begins a return trip traveling back through the original point of rest or equilibrium (point A), and then continues on to the opposite or lower limit (point C). The movement then travels back again returning to the point of equilibrium (point A). This entire voyage completes one cycle. Similarly, one cycle

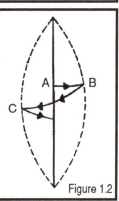

Figure 1.2

in sound consists of a vibration passing by means of compression and rarefaction through every position which encompasses its point of equilibrium (fig. 1.2).

SOME DEFINITIONS

When sound is generated on a musical instrument, the sound presents itself in a symmetrical pattern of vibrations. These vibrations include a fundamental note along with a number of other related notes sounding in lesser degrees of amplitude or volume. The fundamental note alone is a pure tone and can be visualized as a simple wave, free from any accompanying vibrations or tones (fig. 1.3). This type of pure tone is called *sinusoidal* and its image is called

Figure 1.3

a *sine wave*. Pure tones are best produced electronically and are generally considered to be musically uninteresting. When a tone is generated on a musical instrument it is almost always accompanied by a series of related sounds or tones called *harmonics, overtones,* or *upper partials*. (These three terms can be used interchangeably). These harmonics are secondary vibrations occurring concurrently with the fundamental tone and consist of successive multiples of the whole vibrating body. The segments occur as $1/2$, $1/3$, $1/4$, etc. of the original vibrating column and sound with less amplitude than the fundamental (fig. 1.4).

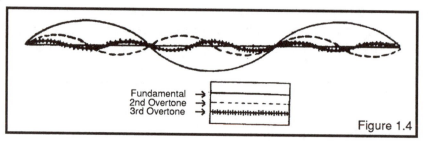

Fundamental →
2nd Overtone →
3rd Overtone →

Figure 1.4

Harmonics are embellishments of the fundamental tone. They are not distinguishable by the listener as entities in themselves but rather serve as an ornamentation to the fundamental. As such, harmonics give a distinctive character to a pitch, allowing the listener to distinguish between the different instruments or voices.

Vibrations per second are commonly referred to as *cycles per second* (abbreviated cps) or *Hertz* (Hz) named after the physicist Heinrich Hertz. The number of Hz refers to a number of complete cycles per second, and so 30 Hz means 30 cycles per second. Any given tone is the product of the number of vibrations or cycles which occur per second, e.g., 'A' 440 is that tone which is produced by a sound generator producing 440 vibrations or cycles per second (fig. 1.5).

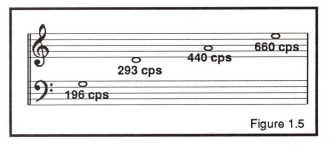

Figure 1.5

Although noise is sometimes used in musical performance, tone is more frequently utilized. It is therefore necessary to understand those attributes of sound production which modify noise, thereby converting it into tone. These attributes are pitch, amplitude and timbre.

Pitch refers to the highness or lowness of tone. The notes of an ascending scale (do, re, mi, fa, sol, la, ti, do) go up in pitch or are successively higher (fig. 1.6). Conversely, in a descending scale (do,

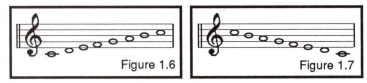

Figure 1.6

Figure 1.7

ti, la, sol, fa, mi, re, do) the notes go down in pitch or are successively lower (fig. 1.7). Any series of notes can take one of only three possible directions in pitch. They can ascend, (fig. 1.8-A) descend, (fig. 1.8-B) or remain the same (fig. 1.8-C).

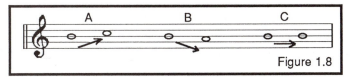

Figure 1.8

Amplitude, a form of energy, refers to the volume or loudness of a sound. Greater amplitude produces louder sounds, whereas less amplitude produces softer sounds. If a sinusoidal curve is used to measure the amplitude of a tone, the amplitude is indicated by the distance from the point of equilibrium to the outermost limit of the sine curve (fig. 1.9).

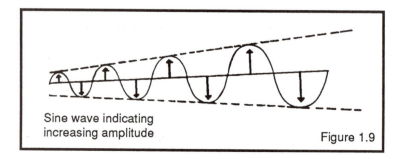

Sine wave indicating
increasing amplitude

Figure 1.9

As is the case with any force, there is a gradual diminution of the energy as it is confronted with resistance such as friction, absorption, or dispersion. With this gradual decline in energy, the tone will gradually dissipate or fade away.

Amplitude (volume) is one of the several physical components that go into the total character of a musical tone. It is the force with which the sound is being produced and is the factor which produces what is commonly referred to as volume or loudness. The more forceful the vibrations per second, the louder the sound. Conversely, the weaker the vibrations per second the softer the sound. Amplitude does not affect pitch. Any pitch can be produced at any amplitude and, therefore, can sound at any volume.

Timbre is the product of the addition of harmonics to a fundamental sound. These additional sounds referred to as *harmonics*, *overtones*, or *upper partials* (see fig. 1.4 above) result from the inherent acoustical characteristics of the sound-producing mechanism, i.e. the instrument producing the sound. For the note C, these sounds follow the harmonic sequence pictured in figure 1.10 and are present in most tones. The same interval pattern would occur for any note. The difference, however, in timbre that is sensed by the listener is the result of the strength (volume/amplitude) of the additional sounds (harmonics) and how they relate in volume to the fundamental. The greater the strength/volume/amplitude of the additional sounds (harmonics) the more intense the nature or timbre of the sound of the instrument. The less the strength/volume/amplitude of

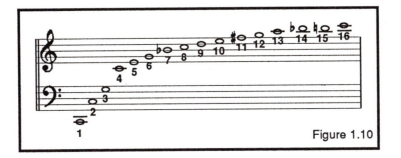

Figure 1.10

the additional sounds (harmonics) the less intense the timbre.

For example, because tones played on an oboe have strong harmonics/upper partials, that instrument produces a tone which can be identified as having an intense timbre. The flute, on the other hand, has a comparatively weak set of harmonics/upper partials, and, therefore produces a more mellow tone.

BIBLIOGRAPHY

SOUND

Apel, W. *Harvard Dictionary of Music*. Cambridge, Massachusetts: Harvard University Press, 1961.

Benade, A. E. *Horns, Strings & Harmony*: Garden City, New York: Anchor Books/Doubleday, 1960.

Donington, R. *Music and Its Instruments*. New York, New York: Methuen, 1982.

Hall, C. J., and E. L. Kent. *The Language of Musical Acoustics.* Elkhart, Indiana: C. G. Conn, 1957.

Peterlongo, P. *The Violin, Its Physical and Acoustical Principles*. New York, New York: Taplinger, 1972.

Stewart, A. *The Music Lover's Guide to the Instruments of the Orchestra*. New York, New York: Van Nostrand Reinhold, 1980.

CHAPTER TWO

THE ANATOMY OF A MUSICAL INSTRUMENT

Musical instruments are devices which have been developed to produce and manipulate sounds. These instruments achieve such a high degree of accuracy that they enable the player to perform an almost infinite variety of music. Although musical instruments are far from perfect, their inventors, developers, and manufacturers have refined their products so as to challenge the potential of even the most gifted performer. We will direct our attention to the technology inherent in these instruments.

Musical instruments function using three basic systems. These are: (1) a sound generating system, (2) a sound amplification system, and (3) a sound manipulating or mechanical key system.

THE GENERATION OF A SOUND

Sound generation systems are different for each category of instrument, and are of five types: three are for woodwind instruments; one for brass instruments, and one for non-fretted string instruments.

Woodwind instruments generate sound by using (1) a *single reed* in conjunction with a mouthpiece (as in a clarinet or saxophone) (2) a *double reed* (as in an oboe or bassoon) or by using (3) a *flat shelf*-like surface positioned so as to allow a stream of air to undulate over and under the edge of the shelf (as in a flute or recorder).

Brass instruments generate sound by having the player's lips buzz within the confines of (4) a *cup-shaped mouthpiece*. This process is common to all brass instruments. It should be noted that there are variations in embouchure and buzzing techniques which apply to the different brass instruments. The basic principle however is the same in all cases.

Non-fretted string instruments (violins, etc.) generate sound by (5) setting *a string into motion* (vibration) either by drawing a bow across the string surface or by plucking the string with the fingers. (There are some alternative methods of generating sound from strings but these are specific to producing special effects and are not relevant to this study).

THE AMPLIFICATION OF A SOUND

A *sound amplification* system complements the sound generating processes described above. The sound produced by the generator alone cannot provide sufficient volume and the timbre to satisfy the musical and esthetic requirements of the listener. These sounds require *a support system* to supply the amplitude necessary for the fundamentals, and their overtones to attain the timbre desired. The support system is in fact *the body of the instrument*. It is the design and construction of the support system in conjunction with the sound generating system that ultimately generate the characteristic sound or timbre of the instrument.

Thus far we have described a device, comprised of a sound producing mechanism coupled with a support system, to provide the amplitude and timbre desired for a specific sound effect. This coupled acoustic system, i.e., the sound source and the associated structure or body of the instrument, still cannot provide a musician with the equipment necessary to produce and manipulate sounds with sufficient variety and versatility to perform music. The coupled device is limited to producing only those sounds which are fundamental to the physical characteristics of the design. Consequently a brass instrument type construction would be capable only of producing those pitches which are the product of the player's adjusting his lip tension or embouchure; a woodwind design would produce essentially the same type of result, and a string instrument would produce only those pitches to which the strings are tuned. It is at this point in the design of an instrument that an *additional system* is necessary. That system must alter the length of the vibrating column so that the pitches which exist between the fundamentals, namely the chromatics, can be added to the fundamental or open tones.

THE MANIPULATION OF A SOUND

We now must add the development of *mechanical systems* such as *valves* and *slides* for brass instruments; *tone holes, ring keys*, and *padded keys* for woodwind instruments; and the *shortening of strings* through the use of fingers of the left hand on the non-fretted string instruments. These systems, added to the basic design of the instrument's body, and joined to a sound source, permit the player to lengthen or shorten the vibrating column of air by small degrees. In so doing the player can produce the pitches which lie between the fundamentals in wind instruments and the tones that exist between the pitches to which the open strings are tuned in the non-fretted string instruments.

As the *vibrating column* of air or the vibrating string is *shortened*, the *pitch is raised*. Conversely, as the vibrating column of air or the vibrating string is *lengthened*, the *pitch* is *lowered*. In the case of *woodwind* instruments, the altering devices take the form of holes in the side of the instrument. Some holes are open and some have padded, cup-shaped keys covering them. As the holes are covered, the instrument becomes longer. If the holes are open, the effective length of the instrument becomes as long as the distance between the sound generator and the first open hole.

Brass instruments have valves or slides which open sections of tubing to lengthen or shorten the vibrating column of air. But on *string* instruments the length of the strings is shortened by pressing (stopping) the string to the fingerboard at any given point with the fingers of the left hand. It is the combination of the sound generator coupled with the body of the instrument and the devices used to alter the length of the vibrating column or string that make a wind or string instrument capable of producing all of the notes that lie within that particular instrument's range.

CHAPTER THREE

THE TRANSVERSE FLUTE

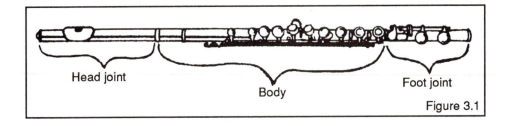

Figure 3.1

The transverse flute (fig. 3.1) provides an excellent model for explaining the generation and modification of sound as well as the material from which musical instruments are made.

This *flute* is made up of *three sections*. These are the *head joint*, (sound generator) the *body*, and the *foot joint* (amplifier). Connected to the body and foot joint is the key system (mechanical system) which ·the player uses to manipulate the fundamental sound that the sound generator and body produce. The sections are joined together by tenons that interlock with each other. The result is an instrument approximately 26½ inches (67.3 cm) long.

The *head joint* of the flute is a slightly tapered tube, stopped at one end with a cork and cap assembly. This tube contains a lip plate into which a tone hole is bored.

The *body* and *foot joint* of the flute together form a cylinder or tube in which there are a number of side holes or tone holes. These are holes in the instrument that can be opened or closed by key mechanisms. The column of air that is set into motion (by the sound generator or head joint) within the body of the instrument will vibrate to the point where the first opening occurs. At that point, the motion is interrupted and the vibrating column ends.

The length of the vibrating column determines the pitch of the tone being produced. The shorter the vibrating column the higher the pitch; conversely the longer the vibrating column the lower the pitch. The performer can shorten or lengthen the tube or body of the instrument by opening or closing the side or tone holes, thereby extending or shortening the vibrating column of air, and consequently changing the pitch.

SOUND GENERATION OF THE FLUTE

In the 1970s a series of experiments led to the conclusion that the *essence of the flute sound* is primarily the product of the material from which the *head joint* is constructed. Additional experiments with varying designs in flute head construction reinforced the finding that the head joint is primarily responsible for the tone quality and that the remainder of the instrument serves merely to amplify and manipulate the sound. This is a particularly important point upon which beginning students of musical instruments should focus, since much time, effort, and money are sometimes devoted to the selection and purchase of instruments made of silver, gold, and platinum in the quest for a better tone quality. Research seems to indicate that excessive attention to that aspect of flute selection is pointless.

Sound is generated on a flute when the player, resting the lip plate against his chin, just below the lower lip, directs a stream of air across the tone hole (fig 3.2). As the stream of air strikes the edge of

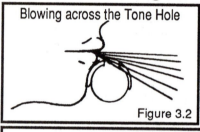

Blowing across the Tone Hole

Figure 3.2

the tone hole opposite the player's lip, the air stream undulates above and below the edge, exciting a pattern of vibrations within the head joint. These vibrations set the air contained within the body of the flute into motion (fig. 3.3). The body then acts as an ampli-

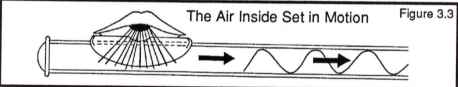

The Air Inside Set in Motion   Figure 3.3

fier for the sound generated in the head joint. This will produce however only that sound which is fundamental to the instrument's design. In order to provide the player with the option of producing an assortment of sounds, the instrument must be designed to enable the player to alter the length of the vibrating column at will and with versatility. This is accomplished by a series of holes which can be opened or closed to lengthen or shorten the vibrating column (fig 3.4).

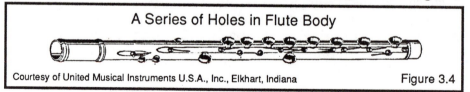

A Series of Holes in Flute Body

Courtesy of United Musical Instruments U.S.A., Inc., Elkhart, Indiana   Figure 3.4

These holes are opened or closed directly by the pads of the fingers or by padded keys controlled by a system of levers (fig 3.5).

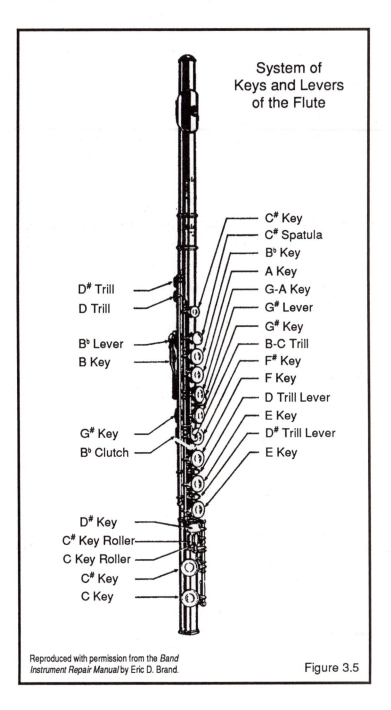

System of Keys and Levers of the Flute

C# Key
C# Spatula
B♭ Key
A Key
G-A Key
G# Lever
G# Key
B-C Trill
F# Key
F Key
D Trill Lever
E Key
D# Trill Lever
E Key

D# Trill
D Trill

B♭ Lever
B Key

G# Key
B♭ Clutch

D# Key
C# Key Roller
C Key Roller
C# Key
C Key

Reproduced with permission from the *Band Instrument Repair Manual* by Eric D. Brand.

Figure 3.5

MECHANISM

The design of *keys on woodwind instruments* has developed in order to *compensate for the limitations of the human hand.* The laws of physics dictate the location and size of the tone holes on the body of an instrument. Unfortunately for musicians, the requirements set by these laws do not coincide with the construction of the human hand, and so in order to fulfill the increasing demand for more notes and greater versatility, mechanical means had to be found to extend the potential span of the fingers. Thus began the introduction of keys for woodwind instruments. Now with the addition of modern *key systems* it is possible for a performer to control the opening and closing of these tone holes regardless of their required location on the body of an instrument. Key systems also allow the player the use of those tones (semitones) which fall between the fundamental tones inherent in the basic construction of the instrument.

Key systems for all woodwind instruments use the same principles of leverage, and are described by the same terminology. There are *two basic types of keys*, the *open* and the *closed.* The terms 'open' and 'closed' are not to be confused with the same terms used to describe the 'open', French, or perforated, and 'closed', plateau, keys of the flute. Musicians believe that open hole (French) keys produce a better sound than the closed hole (plateau) keys since the open design strengthens the upper partials of each note, thereby enriching the sound (fig. 3.6). The term *open key*, when used in the broadest sense, refers to a key which, when at rest, is not covering the hole it services. In effect that hole is open, but it has a key to cover it when necessary (fig. 3.7). The term *closed key*, again when used in its broadest sense, refers to a key which, when at rest, covers and seals the hole it services (fig 3.8). Both of these keys, when activated, produce the inverse effect that their names imply, i.e., when activated, a closed key opens the hole it services whereas an open key closes the hole it services.

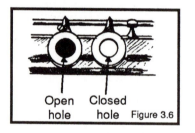

Open hole   Closed hole   Figure 3.6

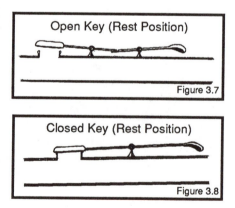

Open Key (Rest Position)

Figure 3.7

Closed Key (Rest Position)

Figure 3.8

Flute *keys* of modern design follow basic principles of leverage using a fulcrum as a pivot point on which the key rocks when activated. There are six parts to a key mechanism. The part in contact with the player's finger is called either the *paddle*, *spatula*, or *finger* (fig. 3.9). On the opposite end of the key is the *pad cup* (fig. 3.9). This cup contains a pad, most often made of felt, which is covered with either leather, fish skin, or sheepskin. The pad covers the tone hole. The paddle and cup are joined by a *stem* (called an *arm*) which in turn is connected to a hollow tube called a *hinge tube* (fig. 3.10). A rod threaded on one end and slotted on the other, (resembling an extended screw) called a *pivot hinge screw*, (fig. 3.11) is inserted through the hinge tube, which is then connected to the stem joining the paddle and pad cup (fig. 3.12). This unit is screwed into two *posts* which are secured to the body of the instrument (fig. 3.13).

The *posts* are attached to the instrument by being screwed directly into the body, soldered onto a plate that is screwed or soldered to the body, or soldered directly to the body of the instrument. A *needle spring* (fig. 3.14) or *flat spring* (fig. 3.15) is used to provide whatever tension is required to return the key to its position of rest after use.

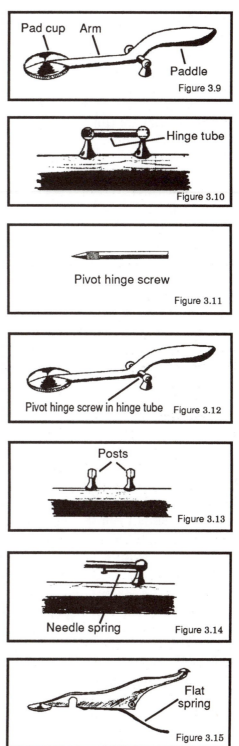

Pad cup Arm
Paddle
Figure 3.9

Hinge tube
Figure 3.10

Pivot hinge screw
Figure 3.11

Pivot hinge screw in hinge tube   Figure 3.12

Posts
Figure 3.13

Needle spring   Figure 3.14

Flat spring
Figure 3.15

Although there are numerous variations, this design is fundamental to all woodwind key systems. Figure 3.5 shows one example of a typical key system and its components.

Tone holes on flutes (and saxophones) extend out from the body, whereas on other woodwind instruments, tone holes are drilled into the instrument's body. The flute tone hole can be constructed independently of the body and then *soldered* onto the body (fig. 3.16)

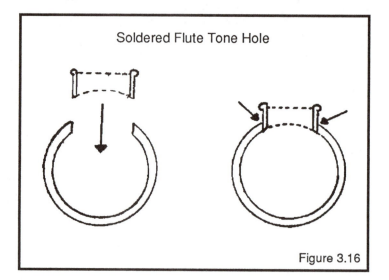

Soldered Flute Tone Hole

Figure 3.16

or it can be *drawn* from the material of the body itself. The process used to construct *drawn tone holes* consists of drilling a small hole in the body of the flute and then pulling a series of balls of increasingly larger size through the hole. The 'drawing' process pulls the material from the inside of the body upward, forming a cup-like projection which extends from the flute body. The resulting projection is then leveled and, in the case of better manufacturing procedures, its edge is rolled, providing a smoother surface on which the pad can rest (fig. 3.17).

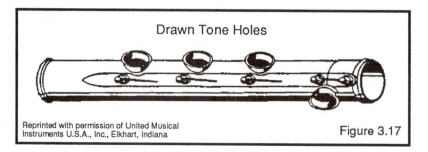

Drawn Tone Holes

Reprinted with permission of United Musical
Instruments U.S.A., Inc., Elkhart, Indiana

Figure 3.17

THE FLUTE FAMILY

A *family of four* flutes is currently in use in contemporary orchestras. The *concert flute* in C (fig. 3.18) is the most common and easily recognizable. This instrument has a prominent role in orchestral, concert band, and marching band repertoire as well as in solo works.

The *piccolo* in C (fig. 3.18) is a small version of the C flute, sounding one octave higher than the C flute. Often used to double the flute and/or violin melodies so as to add a brightness or 'edge' to the sound, the piccolo in C is also used to add an obligato to a selection. This technique can best be heard in some of the more popular marches by John Philip Sousa.

Next in order of descending sound below the C flute is the *alto flute in G* (fig. 3.18). This instrument transposes a fourth lower than the written note. However, it maintains the same written range in the score. The alto flute is not particularly effective in higher register, but in the middle and lower registers it produces a very mellow, rich tone.

At the lowest end of the range of the flute family is the *bass flute in C* (fig. 3.18). This flute sounds an octave lower than the written note while it

Piccolo

Alto flute
in G

Concert
flute

Bass flute
in C

Reprinted with permission of United Musical Instruments U.S.A., Inc., Elkhart, Indiana

Figure 3.18

shares the same written range as the C flute. Because of the extraordinary size of the instrument and the comparatively large size of the embouchure hole in the head joint, many players have a difficult time adjusting to the bass flute after playing the other instruments of the family. A great deal more airflow is required in order to generate the vibrations that excite the air column within the body of the instrument. However, the resulting sound is a rich and haunting tone which is most useful for special effects.

SUMMARY

Sound is generated on the flute through the use of an edge tone, air-reed-type head-joint. The sound generated is *amplified* through the body of the flute and manipulated by a side hole shortening keyed system. The instruments are made of a variety of products ranging from wood through crystal and including numerous metals and alloys. Of greatest importance is the fact that the tone quality of a flute is almost entirely the product of the design. The material used in the construction of the body and keys of the flute has little effect on its tone quality.

This chapter has presented an overview of the physics and mechanics of the modern transverse flute. However, each topic covered can be a major study and should be dealt with in detail if such a quest will serve the needs of the reader.

BIBLIOGRAPHY

THE TRANSVERSE FLUTE

Carse, A. *Musical Wind Instruments*. New York, New York: Da Capo, 1965.

Coltman, J. W. "Acoustics of the Flute." *The Woodwind Anthology*, Volume I. Northfield, Illinois: The Instrumentalist, 1986. (This article, "Acoustics of the Flute," was originally written in 1972.)

Fajardo, R. "Tone Properties of the Flute Head Joint." *The Woodwind Anthology*, Volume I. Northfield, Illinois: The Instrumentalist, 1986. (Article written in 1972.)

Hahn, R. "The Flute Embouchure and the Soda Straw." *The Woodwind Anthology*, Volume I. Northfield, Illinois: The Instrumentalist, 1986. (Article written in 1975.)

Kirmser, L. P. "The Acoustics of the Flute." *National Association of Musical Instrument Technicians*. South Bend, Indiana: Namit, 1977.

Meyer, R. F. *The Band Director's Guide to Instrument Repair*. Port Washington, New York: Alfred Publishing, 1973.

Scribner, G. *The Scribner Guide to Orchestral Instruments*. New York, New York: C. Scribner and Sons, 1983.

Shepard, M. *How to Love Your Flute*. Los Angeles, California: Panjandrum, 1980.

Simpson, M. J. "Spare Not the Rod." *The Woodwind Anthology*, Volume I. Northfield, Illinois: The Instrumentalist, 1986. (Article written in 1972.)

————. "Selecting a Flute." *The Woodwind Anthology*, Volume I. Northfield, Illinois: The Instrumentalist, 1986. (Article written in 1981.)

CHAPTER FOUR

THE CLARINET

The clarinet is a *single reed, closed end,* mostly *cylindrical tube* about 26 inches (66 cm) long. The body of the instrument is not totally cylindrical but instead flares out slightly at its lowest segment to accommodate the *bell,* which continues the flare shape to the end of the instrument. The *mouthpiece* or sound generator is tapered toward the tip so that the entire instrument, although cylindrical for the most part, actually starts off small, but ends up larger.

Most modern clarinets (B♭, or soprano models) are designed to disassemble into *five parts.* These consist of a *mouthpiece* (sound generator), a *barrel, upper* and *lower joints,* and a *bell* which serve as an amplifier (fig. 4.1). There is a *mechanical system of keys* connected to the upper and lower joints. These keys are used by the player to manipulate the fundamental sound produced by the sound generator and amplifier. The purpose of this segmentation is primarily for convenience in packing and carrying, but it also permits the replacement of a single section rather than the entire instrument, should serious damage occur. All of the joints are connected by *cork-covered tenons* which fit into *sockets.*

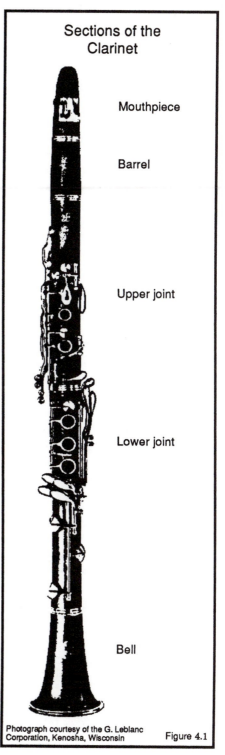

Sections of the Clarinet

Mouthpiece

Barrel

Upper joint

Lower joint

Bell

Photograph courtesy of the G. Leblanc Corporation, Kenosha, Wisconsin

Figure 4.1

The clarinet uses the same system as the flute for lengthening and shortening the vibrating column of air through the use of *side holes and keys with pads* to cover many of those side holes.

One of the unique acoustical characteristics of the clarinet is that its sound production emphasizes the odd numbered overtones as opposed to the more even distribution of overtones present in other woodwind instruments such as the flute, oboe, and saxophone.

The playing range of the clarinet is divided into four sections. The lowest range is called the *chalameau*; above that is the *clarion*, next is the *throat* or *break*, which leads to the highest range, referred to as the *extreme* or *acute* register.

SOUND GENERATION

(THE MOUTHPIECE)

Sound is generated on the clarinet by means of a *single reed* of cane attached to a well designed and carefully constructed mouthpiece. As a player initiates a stream of air flowing through and against the reed/mouthpiece combination, the reed is set in motion, vibrating against the mouthpiece. This excites the column of air within the body of the instrument to vibrate, producing a sound.

Current research in the technology of musical instruments offers voluminous evidence to indicate that the quality of sound produced by an instrument is more the result of the sound generator (in this case the mouthpiece/reed combination) than that of any other factor or combination of factors incorporated in the design or construction of the instrument.

Figure 4.2 shows diagrams of the *clarinet mouthpiece*, indicat-

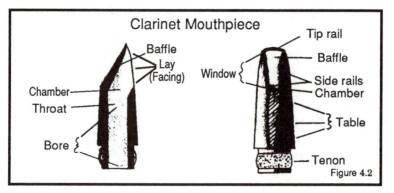

Figure 4.2

ing the names of the parts. The *table* is flat or concave and is the point at which the reed makes contact with the mouthpiece. Above the table is the *facing*. This section is sometimes referred to as the *lay*. This portion is shaped so that it gradually slopes away from the plane of the table. It is at this point that the reed vibrates against the mouthpiece, generating the initial sound. It is the trajectory of this slope that creates the distance that the reed must travel in the course of its vibrations.

On either side of the facing are *side rails*. Although the dimensions of these are not critical, it is absolutely essential that they be identical, neither too wide nor too narrow, and that they have a perfect finish, free of warping or defects of any kind.

The *tip rail* must adhere to the same standards of perfection as the side rails. It is rounded on either side in order to follow the contour of the reed. This part of the perimeter of the window completes the portion of the mouthpiece that makes a seal with the reed. A tip rail of about 1/32 of an inch (.8 mm) is most effective for general use.

The *window* is the space between the rails. It channels the vibrations of the reed to travel into the instrument (amplifier) and to excite the air column in the instrument to produce the tone. The recommended width of the window at the top is slightly less than 1/2 of an inch (11.5 mm).

The *baffle* should measure about 3/8 of an inch and be moderately concave in structure, flattening out as it approaches the tip rail.

The *bore* of the mouthpiece is critical to the tone quality and pitch of the instrument, for it is the point where the mouthpiece, carrying the 'raw' generated tone, meets the bore of the instrument and begins to become tone. As such, it must match the bore of the instrument in order to effectively fulfill its function.

Clarinet mouthpieces have been made of practically every material imaginable. However, over the centuries trial and error have encouraged the industry to settle upon the use of wood, glass (or crystal), plastic, or hard rubber. Although the material used is of some consequence, its importance must be judged in conjunction with other design considerations in making a mouthpiece. Among these are the length of the facing or lay and the size of the opening at the tip. In the broadest terms one might say that extremes in the design of any aspect of the mouthpiece should be avoided, if the designer is to provide for the average student or player. Conversely, at the top level of professional performance a highly specialized design can be obtained through the combined efforts of the performer and the mouthpiece maker. Although there are trends which seem to indicate that certain materials and dimensions are more effective than others for general use, one should bear in mind that all recommendations for such designs must be subject to the needs and physical individuality of the player. These are generalizations, since all rules must allow for exceptions.

AMPLIFICATION

(THE BARREL, JOINTS, AND BELL)

The first phase of the voyage of the column of air that has been excited into motion by the sound generator (i.e., mouthpiece and reed), takes place within the *barrel* of the instrument. The barrel is a short cylindrical section used to join the mouthpiece to the body of the clarinet (fig. 4.1).

Although the original Boehm patent dispensed with the barrel, making the upper joint one piece, the coupler (barrel) has remained a part of all instruments to date. There is some rationale to its persisting, in that it can function as an aid to tuning. The player can extend or contract the overall length of the instrument by moving the barrel slightly in or out of the upper joint. In so doing the instrument is made longer or shorter and the overall pitch lowered or raised respectively.

Of equal importance is the fact that the barrel is the first part of the body of the instrument to receive the flow of warm moist air from the mouthpiece. It is consequently subjected to the greatest amount of expansion and contraction from the constant humidity and temperature changes, which often result in cracking the wood. In such a case a simple replacement of the barrel will resolve the problem as opposed to having to repair or replace the entire upper joint of the instrument.

Following the mouthpiece and barrel, the third and fourth sections of the clarinet are the *upper* and *lower joints*. These are essentially cylindrical in shape, though there is some flaring in the lower joint, starting anywhere from the fourth lowest side hole to the last hole. Flaring is necessary to compensate for the acoustical inconsistencies inherent in the clarinet design.

The *bell* of the clarinet is the lowest portion of the body. This section serves as an extension of the sound amplification system. It also compensates for the absence of subsequent open holes when all holes are closed to play the lowest note on the instrument. When a note other than the lowest one is played, some side holes are closed while the remainder are left open. The first two or at most three of these remaining open holes allow the tone to radiate from the instrument and enhance tone quality and amplification. But when the lowest note on the instrument is reached, these successive open 'amplifying' holes no longer exist causing the tone quality and amplification to suffer. The addition of the bell compensates for the absence of the amplifying holes by acting as an extension of the amplification system.

CHARACTERISTIC SOUND

The *tone quality* or *timbre* of any instrument is a result of the *intensity* of the *overtones* (*harmonics* or *upper partials*) of a tone in relation to the *fundamental* of that tone. (See Chapter 1, p.4 on *timbre*.) The quantity and intensity of these overtones in relation to the fundamental note allow the listener to identify the instrument.

In the case of the clarinet, the even-numbered upper partials (i.e., the second, fourth, sixth, etc.) are present in relatively smaller amplitude as compared to the odd numbered (i.e., the third, fifth, etc.) partials. This imbalance accounts for the characteristic clarinet sound.

MATERIAL

The effect of the material used in constructing a clarinet on the sound it produces is consistent with the findings of those of the flute, i.e. that the material from which the body of the instrument is made has little or no effect on the tone quality. Empirical studies strongly indicate that those involved in the selection of musical instruments, in this case clarinets, should direct most of their attention to the sound-generating aspect of the outfit while giving less attention to the material from which the body is made. This conclusion is of particular importance to those who must consider the cost of the instrument they are buying. As in the case of the flute, the sound generator on the clarinet deserves the greatest investment, while the materials from which the remainder of the instrument is constructed are of less importance.

MECHANISM

The mechanism or key system of the clarinet went through about two centuries of evolution before becoming what is now referred to as the *Boehm* system (fig. 4.3). The fundamental

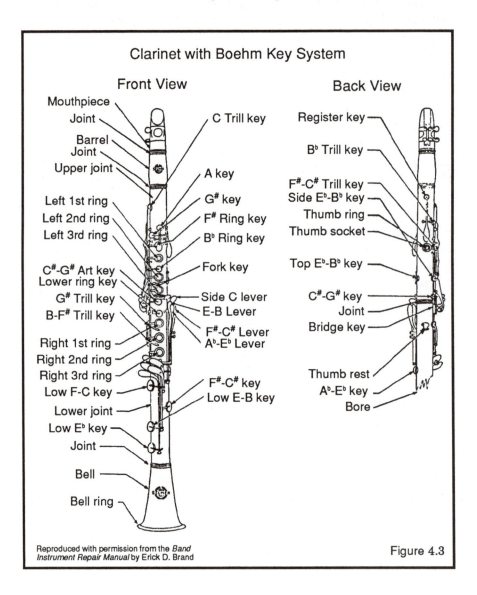

Clarinet with Boehm Key System

Front View — Back View

Front View:
- Mouthpiece
- Joint
- Barrel
- Joint
- Upper joint
- Left 1st ring
- Left 2nd ring
- Left 3rd ring
- C#-G# Art key
- Lower ring key
- G# Trill key
- B-F# Trill key
- Right 1st ring
- Right 2nd ring
- Right 3rd ring
- Low F-C key
- Lower joint
- Low E♭ key
- Joint
- Bell
- Bell ring
- C Trill key
- A key
- G# key
- F# Ring key
- B♭ Ring key
- Fork key
- Side C lever
- E-B Lever
- F#-C# Lever
- A♭-E♭ Lever
- F#-C# key
- Low E-B key

Back View:
- Register key
- B♭ Trill key
- F#-C# Trill key
- Side E♭-B♭ key
- Thumb ring
- Thumb socket
- Top E♭-B♭ key
- C#-G# key
- Joint
- Bridge key
- Thumb rest
- A♭-E♭ key
- Bore

Figure 4.3

systems of leveraged keys, posts, springs, pads, and the like that were discussed in detail in the chapter on the flute apply to the clarinet as well. The plural term 'systems' must be stressed, however, to avoid the impression that the designs of the two instruments are the same. Only the way in which the keys move, interact, and open and close side holes in the body of the instrument is similar on the two instruments. This in fact is true on all woodwind instruments. Beyond that point, the systems must, because of their acoustical individuality, be designed to suit the needs of each instrument.

The modern clarinet is commonly referred to as the Boehm system clarinet. Boehm, however, had little if anything to do with the development and design of the key mechanism. His primary accomplishment was in the determination of the placement of the tone holes so that the laws of acoustics were sufficiently satisfied, producing those sounds now associated with the clarinet. Since Boehm's research required placement of tone holes that rendered playing with the human hand impossible, Hyacinthe-Eleonore Klose, a teacher of clarinet at the Paris Conservatory, and Louis-Auguste Buffet, still a well-known name in clarinet manufacturing, collaborated to invent a key system that would accommodate Boehm's design. Nowadays the Boehm model clarinet has *twenty-four tone holes* that are controlled by *seventeen keys and six rings*. These rings are actually open circles of metal that encircle tone holes. When the tone hole is covered by the player's finger, the ring activates a reciprocal action that in turn covers one or more additional holes.

A careful examination of figure 4.4 will help the reader to visualize and understand the clarinet mechanism as it relates to the Boehm designed body. It should be noted that a number of modifications have been made on the key system—modest additions or design changes primarily intended to facilitate the player's transition from one particular note to another, or to produce a trill that may be particularly awkward to execute.

The Parts of the Body of a Boehm Clarinet

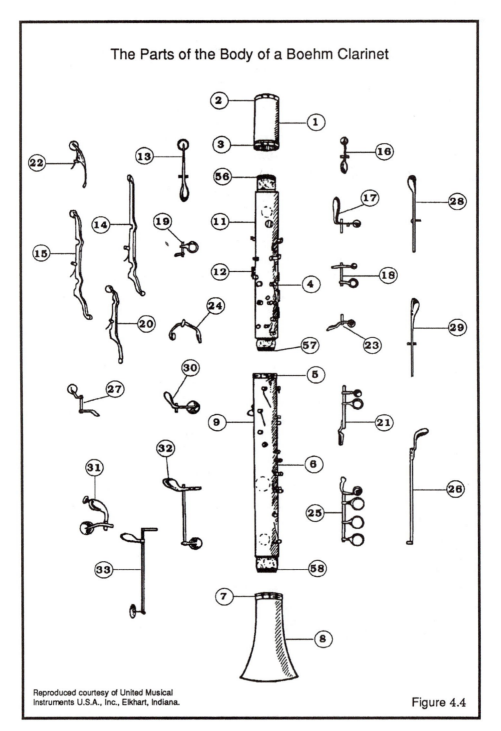

Figure 4.4

Key to Figure 4.4

1 — Barrel joint with rings
2 — Ring, upper barrel joint
3 — Ring, lower barrel joint
4 — Upper joint with post spring
5 — Ring, lower joint
6 — Lower joint with post springs
7 — Ring, upper bell
8 — Bell with rings
9 — Thumb rest
11 — #1 Register vent tube
12 — Insert thumb tube
13 — #1 Register key
14 — #2 Alternate B/C side lever key
15 — B♭ Trill side lever key
16 — Throat A key
17 — Throat G♯ key
18 — #6 F♯/B
19 — #7 F/C Thumb ring key
20 — #8 F♯ Side lever key
21 — #9 D/A Ring key
22 — #12 E♭/B♭ Right side lever key
23 — #13 E♭/B♭ Auxiliary left side lever key
24 — #15 C♯/G♯ Key
25 — #16 Right hand ring key
26 — #17 F/C Left side lever key
27 — #18 Chromatic B/F♯ key
28 — #19 E/B Side lever key
29 — #20 F♯/C♯ Side lever key
30 — #21 A♭/E♭ Key
31 — #22 F/C Key
32 — #23 ALT F♯/C♯ Key
33 — #24 ALT E/B Key
56 — Lower tenon cap
57 — Center tenon cap
58 — Upper tenon cap

THE CLARINET FAMILY

The inventiveness of the human mind has resulted in the creation of numerous clarinets of assorted sizes and transpositions in order to accommodate the player, or to produce special effects. At this time in our musical evolution there are many choices of clarinets which are commonly used. Among them are the A^b and E^b sopranino, B^b soprano, A soprano, F basset horn, E^b alto, B^b bass, EE^b contra-alto, and BB^b contrabass. Figure 4.5 shows a comparison of the sizes and

Representatives of the Clarinet Family

| E^b Soprano Clarinet | B^b Clarinet | E^b Alto Clarinet | B^b Bass Clarinet | BB^b Contrabass Clarinet |

Figure 4.5

general shapes of several members of the clarinet family. For all clarinets, the sound generators, bodies, mechanisms, and acoustical principles are essentially the same. The significant differences are in the size and transposition, and in the shape of the bell and of the coupling devices connecting the mouthpieces to the main bodies of the instruments.

SUMMARY

If the reader will turn back to the concluding remarks in the chapter on the flute and replace the word flute with clarinet, and the term 'head joint' with mouthpiece, the remainder of the comments will apply equally to the clarinet. The studies conducted on the clarinet clearly indicate that the essence of the instrument's sound quality is primarily the product of the sound generator (mouthpiece) and that all that follows serves merely as a means to amplify and manipulate that sound.

The clarinet is acoustically a more complex instrument than the flute in that the clarinet's cylindrical, closed-end design lessens the intensity of the even-numbered overtones in relation to the fundamental, and emphasizes the odd-numbered partials. Since it functions as a closed-end cylinder, as opposed to a closed-end cone, the acoustical balance of nodes and anti-nodes (points of interrupted vibration and of greatest vibration) results in the instrument's overblowing at the twelfth instead of the octave, as do the other woodwinds. This then increases the complexity of the tone hole placement and size, so that accurate intonation relationships among the registers become virtually impossible. The solution is found in placing and sizing the tone holes in such a way that none of the registers is radically out of tune yet never truly in tune.

Although some attempts have been made to alter and improve the shortcomings of the clarinet, change in the music world comes slowly. This tortoise-paced progress is further slowed by the unwillingness of musicians to accept innovation readily.

BIBLIOGRAPHY

THE CLARINET

Backus, J. "Some Experimental Results on the Clarinet." *The Woodwind Anthology*, Volume II. Northfield, Illinois: The Instrumentalist Co., 1986. (Article written in 1964.)

Callahan, W. "Clarinet Mouthpieces: Their Materials and Construction." *The Woodwind Anthology*, Volume II. Northfield, Illinois: The Instrumentalist Co., 1986. (Article written in 1949.)

Carse, A. *Musical Wind Instruments*. New York, New York: Da Capo, 1965.

Donington, R. *Music and Its Instruments*. New York, New York: Methuel, 1982.

Forsythe, C. *Orchestration*. New York, New York: Macmillan, 1949.

Garofalo, R. "Woodwind Instrument Relationships." *The Woodwind Anthology*, Volume II. Northfield, Illinois: The Instrumentalist Co., 1986. (Article written in 1972.)

McCathren, D. "The Effect of Clarinet Mouthpiece Materials on Tone Quality." *The Woodwind Anthology*, Volume II. Northfield, Illinois: The Instrumentalist Co., 1986. (Article written in 1959.)

Rendall, F. *The Clarinet*. W.W. New York, New York: Norton, 1954.

Ritche, R. "The Clarinet Mouthpiece." *The Woodwind Anthology*, Volume II. Northfield, Illinois: The Instrumentalist Co., 1986. (Article written in 1961.)

Sadie, S. *The New Groves Dictionary of Musical Instruments*, Volume I. New York, New York: Groves, 1984.

Stewart, M. *The Music Lovers Guide to the Instruments of the Orchestra*. New York, New York: Van Nostrand Reinhold, 1980.

Tiede, C. *Practical Band Instrument Repair Manual*. Dubuque, Iowa: W. C. Brown, 1970.

CHAPTER FIVE

THE SAXOPHONE

Unlike most other musical instruments, the saxophone was conceived and invented by one individual, Adolph Sax. It was his intention to bridge the gap between the brass and woodwind instrument sections of the orchestra by combining the features of both. The result was a brass instrument with a shortening-hole acoustical design that generated sound by a single reed mechanism similar to that of the clarinet.

Because of Sax's unique, perhaps even radical concept, there was and still continues to be a wide disparity of opinions regarding the virtues and shortcomings of the instrument. Physically, the saxophone can be described as a quasi-inverted, S-shaped, conical brass tube. The tube begins at the mouthpiece, where it is about the size of a dime, and ends up at the bell, where it is about the size of a teacup saucer (fig. 5.1). The saxophone has a range from c' to c" and uses the principle of the shortening-hole system with from 18 to 21 side holes and two vent or octave keys. The saxophone is a hybrid instrument that can produce such a variety of timbres that it belongs in jazz bands and symphony orchestras and can even accompany the human voice.

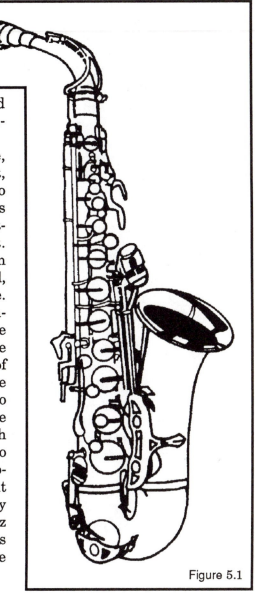

Figure 5.1

SOUND GENERATION

The sound generator of the saxophone is often described in much the same way as the clarinet. On the surface this may seem reasonable. However, a closer inspection shows that some differences have evolved in the mouthpiece over a hundred-and-fifty-odd years, and have proved to be of significant importance. These differences enable it to generate a sound that satisfies the needs of the acoustical design of the instrument.

A vast number of changes have taken place in the design of the saxophone's mouthpiece since its inception in 1840. It has been lengthened, shortened, enlarged, made smaller, cored out, tapered, colored, and re-shaped, using every sort of material conceivable. Each of these changes has contributed to the wide variety of opinions on the sound of the instrument, since each change in mouthpiece design results in a change in tone quality or timbre. In the preceding chapters we noted that the sound generators of the flute and clarinet, i.e., the head joint on the flute and the mouthpiece on the clarinet, were almost entirely responsible for the quality and timbre of the instrument. This is also the case with the saxophone.

The design and names for the parts of the saxophone *mouthpiece* are like those of the clarinet. This explains why it is so easy to make an association with the two and to say simply that the saxophone uses a mouthpiece that is similar to that of the clarinet. The differences, however, are found not in the labels given to the parts nor in the general appearance of the two mouthpieces, but rather in the detail of the specifications of construction.

The *parts* of the saxophone mouthpiece as seen in figure 5.2 are named with much the same terminology as that of the clarinet. The parts are the *bore, window* of the throat, *tone chamber, table, lay* or *facing*, and *baffle*. The *materials* from which the mouthpieces are made are like those used for the clarinet, namely, *wood, glass* or *crystal, plastic,* and *rubber* along with some use of *metal* such as gold and silver.

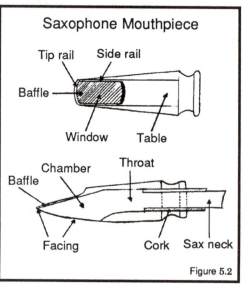

Saxophone Mouthpiece

Tip rail   Side rail

Baffle

Window   Table

Chamber   Throat

Baffle

Facing   Cork   Sax neck

Figure 5.2

Because the saxophone produces tones which include overtones up to the sixteenth partial (greater in number than any other instrument) the tone generator must act not only as a medium to supply sound, but also as a device to control the abundance of sound resulting from the design of the instrument. The early alto saxophone mouthpiece was constructed with a cylindrical bore and with no taper. The throat was round and the tone chamber was not consistent in size but instead had a bulbous portion preceding the window. The wall surfaces were concave, giving it a tone that was mellow and lacked the erasable edge often associated with the saxophone.

The 1930s saw the evolution of the era of the large dance band, and with this era came demand for a sound that would be more compatible with brass instruments. At that time the reeds and brasses were distributed equally in these bands, and it became necessary to strengthen the sound of the reeds to match that of the brasses. Since the sophisticated devices for sound evaluation were not yet available, it was necessary for those involved in research and development to rely on instinct to find remedies. They experimented with materials of various densities and expansion coefficients and redesigned the structure of the mouthpiece interior. This experimentation produced a number of mouthpieces so unsatisfactory that they led to the decline of the reputation of the saxophone as a serious instrument.

During that time one mouthpiece was developed which was a modification of the original and which helped the saxophone regain some of its original popularity. It produced a richer tone with stronger emphasis on the upper partials. Subsequently, the industry developed an additional design modeled on the contours of the clarinet mouthpiece, which became very popular. This mouthpiece produced an extraordinarily powerful and penetrating sound, and it gained favor with those performers of dance band music who were in competition with their brass-playing counterparts. Simultaneously the saxophone was removed from use by classical musicians, due to the instrument's increasing incompatibility with symphonic sounds.

Further experimentation, now with the aid of scientific sound-evaluating devices, led to smaller chambers which proved to be unsatisfactory, and then to the double-tone chamber, which had a tapered cylindrical bore and a smaller tone chamber and throat. This mouthpiece produced a very aggressive sound, enabling a player literally to blast out the notes, but creating a greater likelihood that the less experienced player might lose control of tone quality and intonation.

A mouthpiece that seemed to strike a suitable balance, incorporating most of the attributes mentioned above, in proportions that produced a tone acceptable to most 'classical' musicians, was designed in France. Featuring a round chamber, it produced a smooth, mellow tone yet included sufficient upper partials to still be bright.

Progress in the study of the technology of musical instruments increasingly shows that the instrument's source of sound holds the primary responsibility for the quality of that sound. In other words, the sound generator is the major contributing factor to the quality of the tone produced. For the saxophone, the source of sound (mouthpiece) has proven to be such an extreme example of this position that the player should select the instrument with great care and consideration for aptitude, physical characteristics, embouchure, and playing experience.

AMPLIFICATION

The mouthpiece of the saxophone is coupled to the body or amplifier through an L-shaped neck. The neck serves two purposes. It provides a convenient angle for placement of the mouthpiece in relation to the player's embouchure, and it provides an appropriate placement for the primary octave or vent key. This will be discussed in detail later in this chapter. The main body of the instrument to which the neck is connected is made of brass, is conical in shape, and utilizes a series of side holes. These increase in size as they descend down the main structure. The body ends in an upturned bell with tone holes incorporated almost to the very end of the structure (fig. 5.3).

Since the saxophone is designed as a single, beating-reed, closed-end, conical shaped tube, its acoustical characteristics result in overblowing at the octave and a full production of the overtones in the harmonic series. It can produce a rich, full tone with potential for great flexibility of pitch and timbre limited only by the player's skills. But because the instrument overblows at the octave, it is necessary to divide the air column at the midpoint in order to produce the upper octave. This is achieved through the use of two octave vents, strategically placed to allow for acceptable intonation on all notes (fig. 5.3). Technically, if one were to create a saxophone which played every note in tune, it would be necessary to have an octave vent for each note. The complexity of such a mechanism would make it impractical, and so only two vents are used.

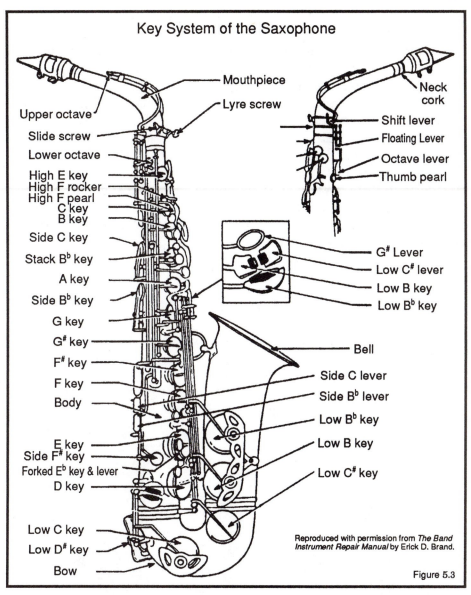

Key System of the Saxophone

Mouthpiece
Lyre screw
Upper octave
Slide screw
Lower octave
High E key
High F rocker
High F pearl
C key
B key
Side C key
Stack B♭ key
A key
Side B♭ key
G key
G♯ key
F♯ key
F key
Body
E key
Side F♯ key
Forked E♭ key & lever
D key
Low C key
Low D♯ key
Bow

Neck cork
Shift lever
Floating Lever
Octave lever
Thumb pearl

G♯ Lever
Low C♯ lever
Low B key
Low B♭ key

Bell
Side C lever
Side B♭ lever
Low B♭ key
Low B key
Low C♯ key

Reproduced with permission from *The Band Instrument Repair Manual* by Erick D. Brand.

Figure 5.3

MECHANISM

The key system of the saxophone uses principles that are similar to those of other woodwind instruments previously discussed. One difference is that the pads on the keys of the saxophone are usually covered with leather instead of with fishskin or sheepskin. This is necessary because the large size of the tone holes and the force of the strike of the key against the tone holes result in increased wear on the pads. The large size also causes the pads to be more susceptible to the accumulation of moisture from the player's breath and makes them subject to more rapid deterioration. Leather pads are stronger and hold up better under these conditions.

The pads described above cover a series of from 18 to 21 side holes. They are graduated in size, starting from the top where the smallest holes are located, to the lowest end of the body where the largest holes are located. The two vent or octave holes (mentioned in a previous paragraph) are located nearest the mouthpiece. The side holes are covered by padded keys, using the same system as the clarinet and flute. When the saxophone is at rest, some of the holes are closed and others are open. To play the instrument, the performer activates the appropriate combination of open and closed holes and manipulates the key system.

THE SAXOPHONE FAMILY

The saxophone family has ten variations of the same instrument. Five are currently in use and should be familiar to any music enthusiast. They are the four shown in figure 5.4 (soprano in B♭, alto

Principal Members of the Saxophone Family

Soprano Sax   Alto Sax   Tenor Sax   Baritone Sax

Figure 5.4

in E♭, tenor in B♭, and baritone in E♭) and in addition the bass in B♭.

The other five variations less commonly used are the sopranino in F and E♭, the soprano in C, the mezzo-soprano in F, the melody in C, and the contrabass in E♭. While all ten instruments belong to the saxophone family, the second five are not readily available, and are not commonly found in the scores of much of today's music.

All of the saxophone models mentioned above are almost identical in fingering and playing requirements. However, adjustments are necessary according to the size of the player. Minor adjustment is also required for embouchure and for simply holding the instrument. These changes are minor however and can easily be adapted to the player. Key systems and fingering are the same, and all instruments are written for in the treble clef in spite of the soprano, alto, tenor, baritone, and bass classifications. Notation is, therefore, identical, and the player can easily switch from one instrument to another without any concern for clef changes.

SUMMARY

The saxophone holds a unique position in the woodwind family for a number of reasons. It is not made of wood but usually of brass (although there have been some made of silver and others of plastic); it is the only single reed, closed end, conical instrument; it overblows at the octave; its tone quality can be radically changed by changing the mouthpiece; its intonation has so wide a range that the experienced player can capitalize on varying the pitch for special effects, (though the amateur has difficulty controlling pitch); and it finds a place in symphony, opera, and jazz either as part of an ensemble or as a solo instrument, all with equal prominence. It has come to be very widely known, and both loved and hated. The saxophone might be considered the only instrument capable of being all things to all people.

The following page contains a diagram (fig. 5.5) of the baritone saxophone taken from the repair parts catalog published by United Musical Instruments U.S.A., Inc., Elkhart, Indiana. The diagram shows a break-down of the instrument, clearly indicating the parts of the body and the key mechanism.

40

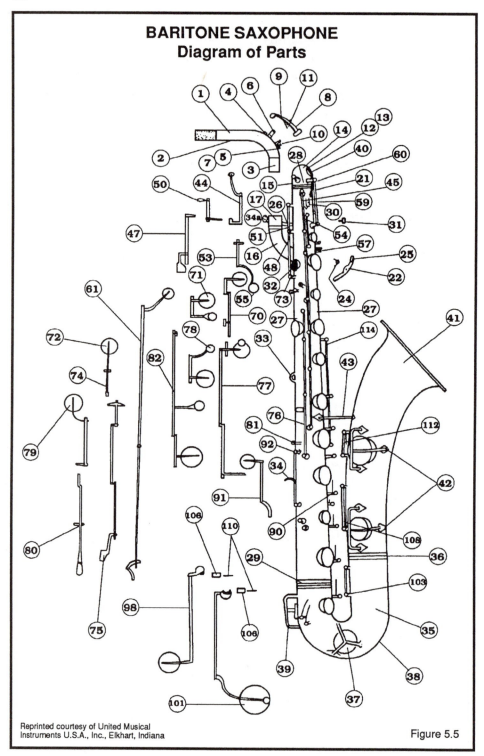

BARITONE SAXOPHONE
Diagram of Parts

Figure 5.5

Key to BARITONE SAXOPHONE Diagram of Parts

1 — Mouthpiece	42 — Guard #21 & #22
2 — Guard Molding	43 — Bell brace
3 — Inside slide	44 — Lower octave key
4 — Octave socket	45 — Hinge screw
5 — Spring box	47 — Octave thumb key
6 — Key guide	48 — Hinge screw
7 — Mouthpiece posts (2)	50 — Octave connection key
8 — Upper octave key	51 — Hinge screw
9 — Flat spring screw	53 — #1 Finger key
10 — Hinge screw	54 — Hinge screw
11 — Flat spring	55 — Felt bumper
12 — Medium & mouthpipe bow	59 — Hinge screw
13 — Medium bow	60 — Spring needle
14 — 6" Guard molding	61 — #2 Key
15 — #4 Octave socket	70 — #5 Key
16 — Mouthpipe bow	71 — #6 Key
17 — Outside slide	72 — #7 Key
21 — #4 Connecting ring (bow)	73 — Hinge screw
22 — Water key	74 — Flat spring
24 — Water key spring	75 — #7 Finger key
25 — Water key cork	76 — Hinge screw
26 — Mouthpipe bow brace	77 — #8 Key
27 — Branch	78 — #9 Key
28 — Ring, medium bow/branch	79 — #10 Key
29 — Ring, branch to bow	80 — #10 Finger key
30 — Music lyre holder	81 — Hinge screw
31 — Lyre holder screw	82 — #11 Key
32 — Thumb rest	90 — Spring needle
33 — Strap ring	91 — #15 Key
34 — Thumb hook	92 — Key guard
34(a) — Screw ligature	98 — #18 Key
35 — Large bow	101 — #19 Key
36 — Bell ring	103 — Hinge screw
37 — 19 Key guard	106 — Finger roller
38 — Guard molding	108 — Hinge screw
39 — 18 Key guard	109 — #21 Finger key
40 — Guard	110 — Roller screw
41 — Bell	112 — Hinge screw

BIBLIOGRAPHY — THE SAXOPHONE

Apel, W. *Harvard Dictionary of Music*. Cambridge, Massachusetts: Harvard University Press, 1961.

Arnold, D. *The New Oxford Companion to Music*. New York, New York: Oxford, 1983.

Benade, A. E. *Horns, Strings & Harmony*. Garden City, New York: Anchor, Doubleday, 1960.

Carse, A. *Musical Wind Instruments*. New York, New York: Da Capo Press, 1965.

Forsythe, C. *Orchestration*. New York, New York: Macmillan, 1949.

Houlik, J. "The Bray of the Sax." *The Woodwind Anthology*, Volume II. Northfield, Illinois: The Instrumentalist Co., 1986. (Article written in 1968.)

Kochnitzsky, L. "Sax and His Saxophone," 1st Edition. New York, New York: Belgian Government Information Center, 1949.

Meyer, R. F. *The Band Director's Guide to Instrument Repair*. Port Washington, New York: Alfred, 1973.

Patrick, L. "The Sax." *The Woodwind Anthology*, Volume II. Northfield, Illinois: The Instrumentalist Co., 1986. (Article written in 1967.)

Patrick, L. "Sax Octave Vents." *The Woodwind Anthology*, Volume II. Northfield, Illinois: The Instrumentalist Co., 1986. (Article written in 1970.)

Rascher, S. "Thoughts about the Saxophone Mouthpiece." *The Woodwind Anthology*, Volume II. Northfield, Illinois: The Instrumentalist Co., 1986. (Article written in 1954.)

Sachs, C. *The History of Musical Instruments*. New York, New York: W. W. North, 1940.

Sadie, S. *The New Groves Dictionary of Musical Instruments*, Volume I. New York, New York: Groves, 1984.

Stauffer, D. *Deficiencies of Wind Instruments in Ensembles*. Washington, DC: Catholic University Press, 1954.

Steinberg, M., and G. Gillis. *Britannica Book of Music*. New York, New York: Doubleday, 1980.

Teal, L. *The Art of Saxophone Playing*. Evanston, Illinois: Summy-Birchard, 1963.

Tiede, C. *Practical Band Instrument Repair Manual*. Dubuque, Iowa: W. C. Brown, 1970.

Willett, W. "The Evolution of the Saxophone Mouthpiece." *The Woodwind Anthology*, Volume II. Northfield, Illinois: The Instrumentalist Co., 1986. (Article written in 1956.)

CHAPTER SIX

THE OBOE

The oboe (fig. 6.1) has the longest list of ancestors of all the woodwinds. Although it resembles the clarinet in appearance, the oboe is in many ways more closely related to the flute and to the saxophone. It is like the flute in their similarity of fingering and in that both overblow at the octave. It is similar to the saxophone in that they both have a conical bore and share similar fingerings.

The oboe is a derivative of the shawm, the most ancient woodwind instrument, and as in the shawm, the sound on the oboe is generated by a *double reed* which excites a column of air contained within a conical tube. The tube can be made of a variety of hardwoods, plastic or, in rare instances, metal. The *body* (amplifier) consists of three parts, and uses the *side-hole-shortening principle* combined with the mechanical principles of key systems found on all of the other woodwind instruments. The exception with the oboe is that there are four different key systems currently in use. These have different levels of complexity, the more complex ones allowing the player greater versatility. The oboe produces a resonance that is rich in upper partials resulting in an intense tone. It is the closed-end, conical design of the instrument that causes it to overblow at the octave and to require fingering similar to that of the flute and the saxophone.

Figure 6.1

Reprinted with permission of
The Selmer Co., L. P.
P.O. Box 310, Elkhart, Indiana

SOUND GENERATION

The oboe has *no mouthpiece*. Its sound generator takes the form of a *double reed*, i.e. two cane reeds bound together onto a metal tube called a staple. The staple is covered with cork and joins the reed to the body of the instrument. When the reed is placed between the player's lips and air is blown into the special ()-shaped opening that is formed by the two blades of the reed, the blades vibrate against each other, activating the air column already present in the body of the instrument. The sound produced is then modified by the body and keys of the instrument (fig. 6.1). A single-reed mouthpiece resembling a small version of the clarinet's mouthpiece will be discussed later in this chapter.

The oboe reed is simple in design. It is, however, the subject of much dismay, frustration, conflict, and despair among oboists. The sound generators of other instruments may be easily obtained, but oboists cannot go to the local music dealer and select a mouthpiece from an assortment of designs, materials, sizes, and shapes. Oboists are condemned either to make their own sound generators (which will, incidentally, have a relatively short life) or to depend on a reed maker for a steady supply. This dependence is unique to oboe players and to other players of double-reed instruments. Although single reed users also suffer anguishes related to reed usage, their plight is less serious than that of the double reed user, as it is the mouthpiece of the single reed instrument and not the double reed itself that plays the most significant role as the true sound generator.

On the oboe, the only source of sound production is the double reed which, being constructed of cane, is by its very nature inconsistent. Each reed is unique in its structure. Even the same instrument played by the same performer can never exactly reproduce a given tone quality when a different reed is used. One attempt at circumventing the inconsistence of the double reed was the introduction of the *single reed mouthpiece* designed for use on a double reed instrument (fig. 6.2). This mouthpiece copies the general structure and design of a clarinet mouthpiece, but is adapted to the size and needs of an oboe or bassoon. The purpose of the device is to enable a clarinet player to double on the oboe in a 'pinch'. When the music requires a short passage for an oboe, and the budget does not allow an oboist to be hired for this, the single reed mouth-piece can be used. The single reed oboe (or bassoon) mouthpiece is also very convenient for younger students who are usually not musically or physically mature enough to deal with all of the challenges of using a double reed.

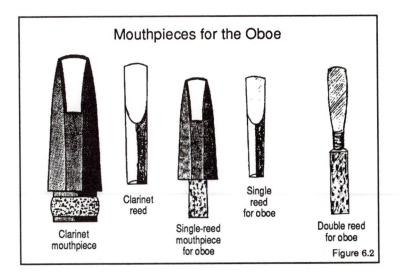

Mouthpieces for the Oboe

Clarinet mouthpiece

Clarinet reed

Single-reed mouthpiece for oboe

Single reed for oboe

Double reed for oboe

Figure 6.2

The use of the single-reed mouthpiece on the oboe has stirred much controversy. It is this writer's opinion that there is a place for the mouthpiece in the overall scheme of music performance and that, given certain circumstances, such a device can prove to be useful and can possibly even 'save the day'. Pragmatic but sparing use of any device which will extend the performance of music to those who need such aids is certainly advisable. But the user must also bear in mind that the single-reed oboe mouthpiece is not a permanent substitute for the original sound generator, i.e. the double reed.

An in-depth look at oboe reeds requires complex and lengthy research, and leads to inconclusive results. Writings by experts who specialize in the area of oboe sound production indicate that there are still no definitive recommendations regarding what will produce the best sound on a double-reed instrument. There are still no final answers. If the topic is of particular interest, the reader may wish to undertake a special study of double reeds and the problems associated with their construction and use.

AMPLIFICATION

The body of the oboe functions as the amplifier for the sound generated by the reed. As mentioned previously, the *body* of the oboe is conical in shape and usually constructed of hard wood or plastic. It is designed with a side-hole system and a *key mechanism* consisting of levers, cups, and pads similar to, but more complicated than that of the clarinet.

The *bore* of the oboe is *conical* in shape. The cone, starting at the staple or point of entry of the reed, is small in comparison with other woodwind instrument bores. Being conical and closed-ended, the oboe overblows at the octave. Because the cone is so small, it produces a *tone* that is rich in upper partials in relation to the fundamental. In fact, the instrument is capable of producing as many as *twelve or more partials*. These partials are extremely intense and in some cases are even capable of overpowering the fundamental. This is not to say that the fundamental is not audible to the listener, for the human ear, in conjunction with the central nervous system, is able to distinguish the intended pitch in spite of the ratio of the fundamental to its partners in sound.

The oboe's small conical bore and proportionately small side holes, in conjunction with the intense nature of a double-reed sound generator, produce an intense spectrum of overtones above a fundamental. The timbre produced is reedy and intense, the sound that is distinctive of and peculiar to the oboe.

MECHANISM

Unlike the saxophone which was invented and built by one man, the oboe evolved over centuries. During the past century and a half, a number of different key systems were tried in attempts to maximize the potential of the basic conical double-reed instrument. These were simple systems such as a thumb plate system, nonautomatic octave keys, low B-C connections, an articulated E^b, a forked-F vent, an articulated G$^\#$, thumb plate action; a half-hole plate, a semiautomatic octave key, and a full automatic octave key. Other devices were added to and subtracted from the key system of the oboe in France, Germany, England, Spain, and other countries. The various key systems that were developed enjoyed varying degrees of success and longevity.

All of the above evolved into what is now referred to as the *conservatory system* developed by Lucien Lorée and George Gillet during the years between 1900 and 1906 (fig. 6.3). Today it is generally referred to as the *plateau* or *French system*. But in fact the saga does not end there, for there are a number of variations of this system. These are the basic conservatory, modified conservatory, standard conservatory, and full conservatory models. They are all basically modifications of the original design of Lorée and Gillet.

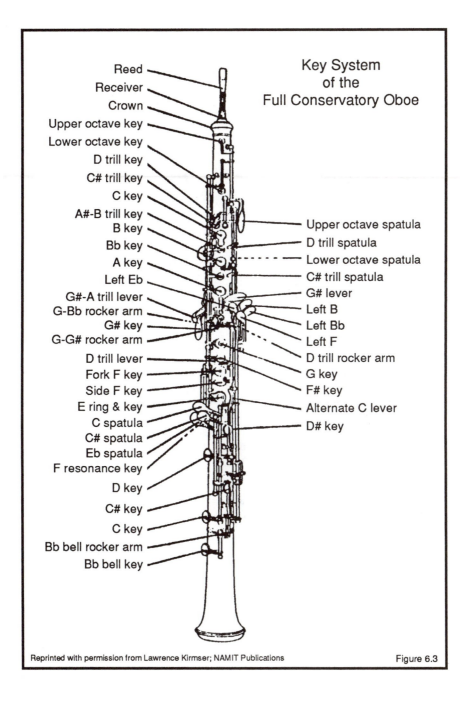

Reed
Receiver
Crown
Upper octave key
Lower octave key
D trill key
C# trill key
C key
A#-B trill key
B key
Bb key
A key
Left Eb
G#-A trill lever
G-Bb rocker arm
G# key
G-G# rocker arm
D trill lever
Fork F key
Side F key
E ring & key
C spatula
C# spatula
Eb spatula
F resonance key
D key
C# key
C key
Bb bell rocker arm
Bb bell key

Key System
of the
Full Conservatory Oboe

Upper octave spatula
D trill spatula
Lower octave spatula
C# trill spatula
G# lever
Left B
Left Bb
Left F
D trill rocker arm
G key
F# key
Alternate C lever
D# key

Reprinted with permission from Lawrence Kirmser; NAMIT Publications

Figure 6.3

Figure 6.4 presents a brief description of the different systems in chart form.

Figure 6.4—Numbers and Types of Keys Found on Oboe Key Systems						
System	No. of Keys	Plateau	Range	Trill	Bell	Other
Basic Conservatory	15	6	low B	F#-G# D♭-E♭ Hi C-D Hi B-C	no	
Modified Conservatory	16	6	low B♭	same + A♭-B♭	yes	forked F resonance key
Standard Conservatory	18	6	low B♭	same + G#-A C-C# D#-E	yes	same
Full Conservatory	19	6	low B♭	same + low B-C#	yes	left hand F

A point of interest to the music educator is that in spite of the preference for plateau keys by professional performers, the *ring type key* (similar to that found on the clarinet) is recommended for school use. The ring system is less likely to go out of adjustment and is found to be more suited to the physical stress to which a school instrument may be subjected.

The final reference to the oboe key system deals with its insatiable desire to be adjusted. Due to the complexity of the system and the variety of possible assorted accessory keys, the instrument can have as many as seventeen adjustment screws. Each of these adjustments regulates two or more keys so that their reciprocal function will be operational.

THE OBOE FAMILY

In addition to the oboe in C there are four other similar instruments often referred to as 'deep oboes'. These are the *oboe d'amore* in A, the *cor anglais* or *English horn* in F, the *bass oboe* in low C and the *heckelphone* in low C. The cor anglais and heckelphone are depicted in figure 6.5 for comparison with the oboe in C. It is important to note that all of these instruments transpose below the oboe in C by the interval of the key named. They share almost all of the characteristics of the oboe in C, using a double reed on a conical amplifier controlled by a complex key system over a side-hole system. In addition to their varying ranges, the significant differences are in the transpositions and the addition of a metal crook at the top and a bulbous bell at the bottom.

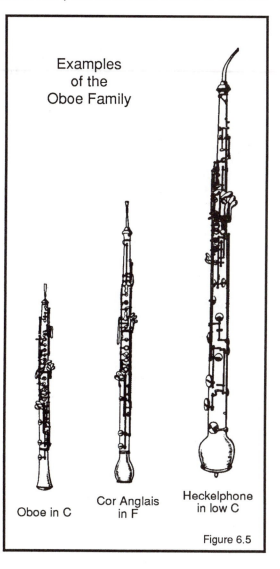

Examples
of the
Oboe Family

Oboe in C

Cor Anglais
in F

Heckelphone
in low C

Figure 6.5

SUMMARY

The *oboe* comes from one of the oldest methods of wind instrument music-making. It evolved from the primitive act of squeezing together the ends of a cut reed, and blowing air through the small space remaining to excite a vibration. It is now one of the most complicated woodwind instruments, produces sounds of great intensity and is regarded by many as one of the most sophisticated of the modern orchestral instruments. It is challenging to learn, difficult to play, expensive to purchase, and demanding in its maintenance requirements, but still the tonal jewel of the ensemble.

BIBLIOGRAPHY

THE OBOE

Banade, A. *Horns, Strings and Harmony*. New York, New York: Doubleday, 1960.

Bains, A. *Woodwind Instruments and Their History*. New York, New York: W. W. Norton, 1963.

Forsythe, C. *Orchestration*. New York, New York: Macmillan, 1949.

Hendrick, P. "On Beginning Oboe Players." *The Woodwind Anthology*, Volume I. Northfield, Illinois: The Instrumentalist Co., 1986. (Article written in 1969.)

Kaplan, J. "Coping with Commercial Oboe Reeds." *The Woodwind Anthology*, Volume I. Northfield, Illinois: The Instrumentalist Co., 1986. (Article written in 1984.)

Mayer, R. "Making Our Own Reeds for Oboe." *The Woodwind Anthology*, Volume I. Northfield, Illinois: The Instrumentalist Co., 1986. (Article written in 1953.)

McGann, D. "The Effect of Saliva on Reeds." *The Woodwind Anthology*, Volume I. Northfield, Illinois: The Instrumentalist Co., 1986. (Article written in 1976.)

N.A.M.I.T. (Section B) "Oboe/English Horn." *National Association of Musical Instrument Technicians*. South Bend, Indiana: NAMIT Publications, 1977.

Probasco, R. "Preparing The Oboe Reed for Playing." *The Woodwind Anthology*, Volume I. Northfield, Illinois: The Instrumentalist Co., 1986. (Article written in 1974.)

Russell, M. "Single or Double Reeds for Oboe?" *The Woodwind Anthology*, Volume I. Northfield, Illinois: The Instrumentalist Co., 1986. (Article written in 1955.)

Sachs, C. *The History of Musical Instruments*. New York, New York: W. W. North, 1940.

Sadie, S. *The New Groves Dictionary of Musical Instruments*, Volume I. New York, New York: Groves, 1984.

Wilson, M. "In Tune With Oboe Intonation." *The Woodwind Anthology*, Volume I. Northfield, Illinois: The Instrumentalist Co., 1986. (Article written in 1979.)

CHAPTER SEVEN

THE BASSOON

The bassoon is the *lowest pitched* of the double reed instruments. (The contrabassoon is lower, but is really another form of bassoon). In theory the bassoon shares many of the historical, physical, and mechanical characteristics of the oboe. It is a descendent of the *shawm*; it is a *closed-end* instrument that generates sound by using a *double reed*. The body of the instrument (sound *amplifier*) has a *conical bore* and uses a *side-hole shortening system* implemented by a mechanical padded key system like that of all other woodwind instruments. Considering all of the above, is the bassoon simply a large oboe? The answer is no. Bassoons are considered by many to be acoustical enigmas and, as such, are the instruments most challenging to understand, to build and to play.

A bassoon is a conical woodwind instrument about 8 feet (2.5 m) long (fig. 7.1).

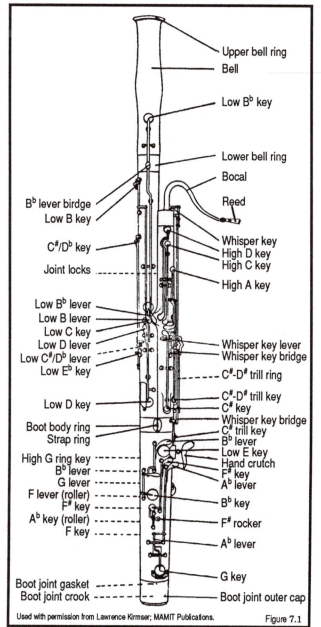

Upper bell ring
Bell
Low B♭ key
Lower bell ring
Bocal
Reed
B♭ lever birdge
Low B key
Whisper key
High D key
High C key
C♯/D♭ key
Joint locks
High A key
Low B♭ lever
Low B lever
Low C key
Low D lever
Whisper key lever
Low C♯/D♭ lever
Whisper key bridge
Low E♭ key
C♯-D♯ trill ring
C♯-D♯ trill key
Low D key
C♯ key
Whisper key bridge
Boot body ring
C♯ trill key
Strap ring
B♭ lever
High G ring key
Low E key
B♭ lever
Hand crutch
G lever
F♯ key
F lever (roller)
A♭ lever
F♯ key
B♭ key
A♭ key (roller)
F lever
F♯ rocker
A♭ lever
G key
Boot joint gasket
Boot joint crook
Boot joint outer cap

Used with permission from Lawrence Kirmser; MAMIT Publications.

Figure 7.1

It is separated into five sections that are assembled by the use of the tenon design, similar to that used in the clarinet and oboe. The first and smallest section of the bassoon is the *bocal* (fig. 7.2). Made of

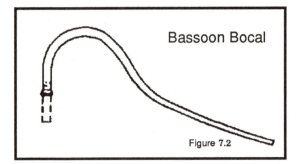

Bassoon Bocal

Figure 7.2

metal, it serves as the receiver for the reed and connects that sound generator (reed) to the body of the instrument. The bore at the bocal is about $\frac{1}{8}$ of an inch (3 mm) in diameter. The bore progresses through the body or amplifier which consists of the *wing joint, boot joint, bass joint, and bell joint.* The bore ultimately reaches a final diameter of about $1\frac{1}{2}$ inches (3.8 cm) at the bell. These sections of the bassoon are *usually made of maple*, although other woods—sometimes ebonite, and occasionally metal—are used.

Because the bassoon is about eight feet long, it is folded in half at about the midpoint by the use of a U-bend called the *boot*. Bassoons are now made in two types, the *long-bore* and *short-bore* models. The *long bore* instrument produces a darker tone and is believed by many to produce truer intonation. The short bore bassoon is more difficult to control and, therefore, is less consistent in its intonation.

An interesting aspect of the design of the bassoon is that the rate of expansion of the bore is half that of the oboe. Another design feature peculiar to the bassoon is that the tone holes at some points need to travel as far as 2 inches (5 cm) to reach the bore. These must be drilled at an angle so that the bore end of the hole will be positioned to achieve the pitches desired and yet enable the player to span the distance with the fingers on the exterior of the body (fig. 7.3). This particular requirement results in a weakening of the venting (interrupting the vibrating column of air), which allows a great portion of the energy to travel to the lower section of the instrument. The result is the strong resonance that is so peculiar to the sound of the bassoon.

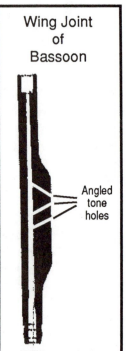

Wing Joint
of
Bassoon

Angled tone holes

Figure 7.3

There are presently two different models or designs of bassoons in use. These are the *French* and the *German*. The difference is primarily in the key mechanism and will be explained later.

SOUND GENERATION

The sound generator for the bassoon is the *double reed*. Like the oboe, the bassoon has no mouthpiece and so it shares all of the problems of sound generation discussed in the previous chapter on the oboe, but with a few additions. Bassoon reeds, like oboe reeds, are *consistently inconsistent*. One can expect that no two reeds will be alike. Therefore, there will be no two reeds producing exactly the same sound even though they are used by the same performer and on the same instrument. This is because the reeds are individually made by hand and are subject to the limitations of the maker. In addition, the raw material, cane, is by its very nature lacking in consistency, and is so delicate that the life span of a bassoon reed is relatively short. This combination of factors creates a potential for problems of sound generation on the bassoon that require much dedicated attention and expertise.

Bassoon reeds are made in a variety of sizes, shapes, densities, and designs. There are about ten parts to the design or shaping of the reed. If one were to multiply the number of variables by the number of parts where those variations might occur, the likelihood of arriving at a clinical description of what a bassoon sound generator is, becomes almost impossible. It is, however, possible to bring an awareness to the reader of the design, structure, fabrication process, and assorted possible styles of reeds commonly in use. This information can serve as a base from which to work in developing opinions and for gathering additional knowledge on the subject.

Figure 7.4 is a diagram of the parts of a bassoon reed showing its two major sections. The *tube*, (consisting of the parts of the lower portion indicated by a bracket and dotted lines), starts at the shoulder and

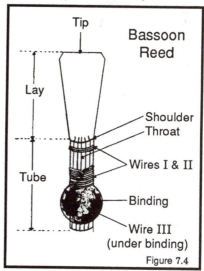

Tip

Bassoon Reed

Lay

Shoulder
Throat

Wires I & II

Tube

Binding

Wire III
(under binding)

Figure 7.4

contains the *first wire*, (sometimes the references to first and second wire are reversed), the *throat,* or *second wire*, and the binding, under which there is a third wire. The upper half of the reed, called the *lay*, consists of the vibrating portion of the reed and includes the tip which is the most sensitive portion of the reed.

Bassoon reeds, like the instruments they serve, are classified as being either *German* or *French* in construction. The difference between them is primarily in the thickness of the lay or heart of the reed. German reeds tend to be thicker in the heart, whereas the French reed has a more gradual and even taper. This difference can be seen by holding the reed up to a strong light. One will notice that the center of the lay is shadowed on the German reed, whereas on the French reed the light passes through evenly (fig. 7.5 and 7.6). This difference can also be felt by gently passing the heart of the reed between the thumb and index finger. The German reed will have a bulge down the

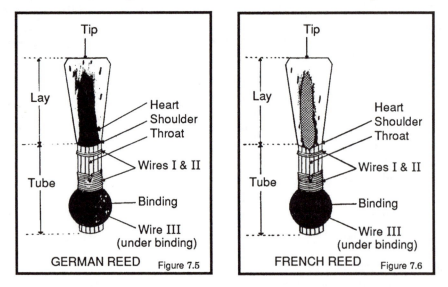

center of the lay, while the French reed will feel flat. As a result of this structural difference, the French reed produces a thinner, more penetrating sound, while the German reed has a more haunting and darker sound.

The next aspect that must be considered when examining the reed of a bassoon is the *longitudinal contour of the lay*. There are *three* possible contours which are used in double reed manufacture. These are the *parallel contour*, the *wedge type*, and the *double-wedge contour* (fig. 7.7). The parallel contour (1) is constructed so that both blades are of equal thickness throughout. This design is not com-

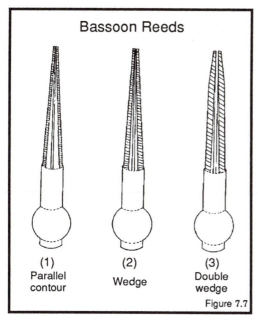

Bassoon Reeds

(1)
Parallel
contour

(2)
Wedge

(3)
Double
wedge

Figure 7.7

monly used, for it is difficult to make, and presents a problem to the player in maintaining control of pitch and tone quality. The wedge contour (2), where the blades gradually taper or thin out toward the tip, is used primarily in the construction of the French style reed. This design is more popular and easier to fabricate. The double-wedge contour (3), used primarily for the German design reed, has many variations, because it uses two degrees of taper. The first section of the blades shows a very slight taper or, sometimes, none at all. The second section of the blades then tapers more abruptly toward the tip of the reed. The length of the two sections of taper can vary significantly, according to the needs of the player and the design used by the reed maker.

AMPLIFICATION

The bassoon *body* (amplifier) is closed end and conical with side-hole pitch control and a key system similar in action to that of the other woodwind instruments. As such, the instrument enjoys all of the attributes of the oboe. One significant difference between the two instruments however, is that the bassoon is much larger in size, about eight feet long. This difference poses a problem because such a long tube must be adapted to be easily handled. The acoustical requirements of such a large instrument dictate that the spacing of tone holes be beyond what the human hand can span.

The problem of size was dealt with by folding the instrument in half. Using a *boot* at the bottom (fig. 7.8), the lengthy body was made more manageable. In order to compensate for the last bit of length and to provide a convenient device for minor tuning adjustments, a *bocal* (or set of different size bocals) was added at the top (fig. 7.9).

58

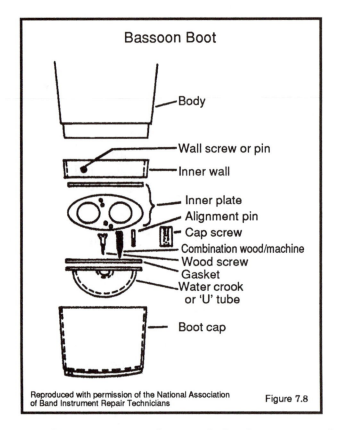

Bassoon Boot

Body

Wall screw or pin

Inner wall

Inner plate
Alignment pin
Cap screw
Combination wood/machine
Wood screw
Gasket
Water crook
or 'U' tube

Boot cap

Figure 7.8

The acoustical requirements for tone hole placement, which was beyond the reach of the normal human finger span, were solved by drilling the tone holes so that they traveled through the body at an angle. This allowed the holes to be placed at a closer proximity to each other on the outside of the body, while being further apart at the bore of the instrument (fig. 7.3). The angular drilling of the holes results in some sacrificing of tone quality.

Due to its length, the body of the bassoon must be folded in half, causing the air column to travel around a U-shaped bend, and hindering to some degree the flow of the vibrating column of air. This lengthy column of air must be supported by the principle of *reinforced resonance through segmentation*. Using this principle, the segments of the vibrating column within the bore of the instrument are reinforced by gradually being introduced to the atmosphere through the use of *speaker holes* (half holes or vents). These openings are located so that they service the initial portion of the upper register.

The design of the key system for the basoon is illustrated on the following pages in figures 7.9 and 7.10.

BASSOON

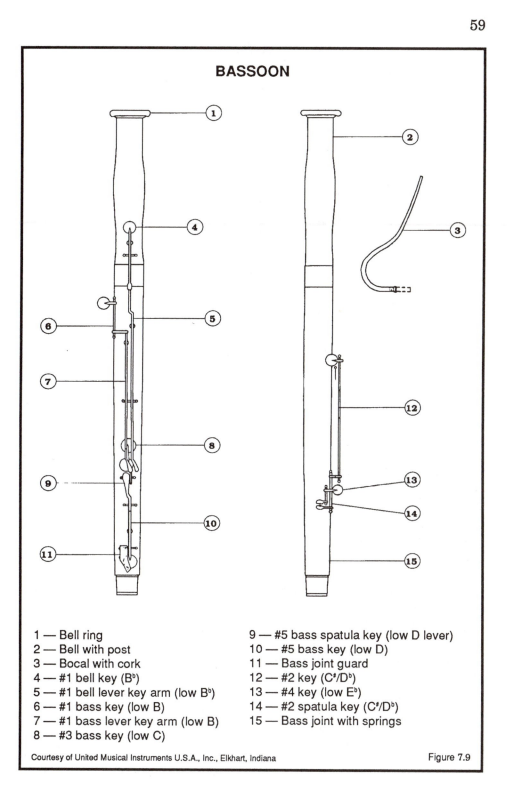

1 — Bell ring
2 — Bell with post
3 — Bocal with cork
4 — #1 bell key (B♭)
5 — #1 bell lever key arm (low B♭)
6 — #1 bass key (low B)
7 — #1 bass lever key arm (low B)
8 — #3 bass key (low C)

9 — #5 bass spatula key (low D lever)
10 — #5 bass key (low D)
11 — Bass joint guard
12 — #2 key (C♯/D♭)
13 — #4 key (low E♭)
14 — #2 spatula key (C♯/D♭)
15 — Bass joint with springs

Figure 7.9

BASSOON

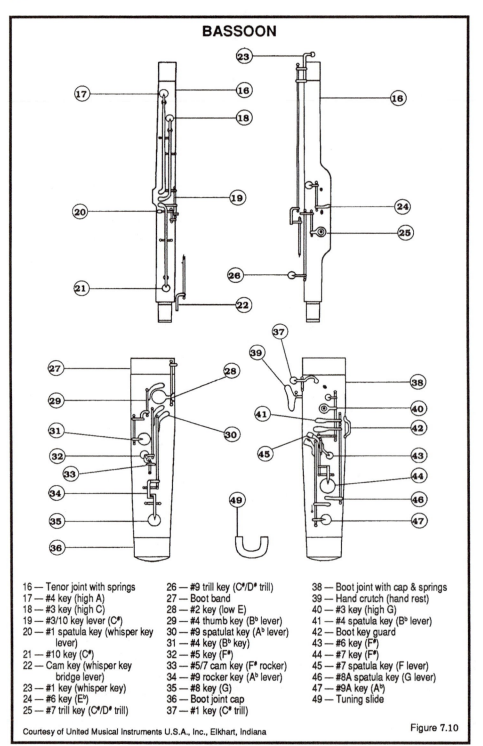

16 — Tenor joint with springs
17 — #4 key (high A)
18 — #3 key (high C)
19 — #3/10 key lever (C#)
20 — #1 spatula key (whisper key lever)
21 — #10 key (C#)
22 — Cam key (whisper key bridge lever)
23 — #1 key (whisper key)
24 — #6 key (E♭)
25 — #7 trill key (C#/D# trill)

26 — #9 trill key (C#/D# trill)
27 — Boot band
28 — #2 key (low E)
29 — #4 thumb key (B♭ lever)
30 — #9 spatulat key (A♭ lever)
31 — #4 key (B♭ key)
32 — #5 key (F#)
33 — #5/7 cam key (F# rocker)
34 — #9 rocker key (A♭ lever)
35 — #8 key (G)
36 — Boot joint cap
37 — #1 key (C# trill)

38 — Boot joint with cap & springs
39 — Hand crutch (hand rest)
40 — #3 key (high G)
41 — #4 spatula key (B♭ lever)
42 — Boot key guard
43 — #6 key (F#)
44 — #7 key (F#)
45 — #7 spatula key (F lever)
46 — #8A spatula key (G lever)
47 — #9A key (A♭)
49 — Tuning slide

Courtesy of United Musical Instruments U.S.A., Inc., Elkhart, Indiana

Figure 7.10

MECHANISM

As stated above, there are two different types of bassoons currently in use, the *German system* and the *French system*. Though the instruments are similar in appearance, there are considerable differences in the number of keys and how they are utilized. It should be noted at this point that the manner in which the keys function is for the most part the same as that of the other woodwind instruments. Padded cups cover holes, and the cups are interconnected and controlled by the player's depressing spatulas or finger plates. Posts, pivot screws, screw rods and tubes, needle springs, and flat springs are all present in some form, and all of these conform to the descriptions of the key systems in earlier chapters.

In spite of all the similarities of design, there remains one profound difference between the French and German key systems. The *German* system bassoon contains many more keys especially in the boot joint. Specifically, the German system, (sometimes referred to as the *Heckel system*, after the family of the same name that owns the world's most famous bassoon factory) will contain from *twenty-one to twenty-four keys*, depending on the sophistication of the model being examined. Additional features are assorted rollers to facilitate a smooth transition from one key to another, an automatic whisper key, assorted trill keys, ring keys, key guards, joint locks, extension up to high E and low AA below the fundamental B♭, posts and springs that are locked in place with screws, metal-lined tone holes, extra octave keys, and half-hole keys such as those found on the oboe. All of the extras on this rather lengthy list— although they are 'extra' only in the sense that a bassoon could be played without most of them—are available on the Heckel, or German model bassoon. They facilitate the playing of the instrument and improve its intonation and life span. These parts are fabricated of nickel silver, German silver, or brass.

The *French* key system on the other hand permits the player to perform the same music, but the system is mechanically simpler and relies more on the player's virtuosity to achieve the transitions from note to note. The French instruments also contain trill keys, finger plates and rings, rollers, and

SUMMARY

The bassoon provides the lowest notes of the woodwind choir. Considered by some to be the clown of instruments because of its ability to produce sounds that can evoke humor in the musical psyche, it is far from humorous in its design or the demands it places on its players. On the opposite side of the spectrum is its ability to transmit a solemnity, graphically demonstrated in the opening measures of Tchaikovsky's Sixth Symphony, the Pathetique. In spite of the bassoon's large size, the successful work of its developers has made it possible to manipulate it musically. There are many passages that are impressively rapid and complex and which can be performed confidently and competently by the professional bassoonist.

Technologically speaking, the instrument is consistent with its woodwind relatives in terms of the maintenance demands of its sound generator, sound amplifier, and key work. The only possible exception might be that the keys are long and numerous and, therefore, may need more frequent regulation.

Considering the acoustical and technological complexities created by the use of a double reed on a large, conical, closed-hole instrument, it appears that the bassoonist must function in an atmosphere of compromise if the instrument is to respond effectively. The bassoon cannot operate for more than one octave without sacrificing quality, and so the reed, which cannot be changed in mid-passage, must be designed so that it will function reasonably effectively in all registers, at the expense of not being at its best in any one given register.

Does this mean that becoming involved with a bassoon as a technician or a performer is indeed to make a commitment to a life of challenge and frustration? This may be one of the areas of musical instrument technology for an aspiring technician to make a mark in the industry. Such ambition might accomplish redesign of the bassoon so that it will produce the unique sound for which it is known without all of the negative characteristics inherent in the present instrument.

BIBLIOGRAPHY

THE BASSOON

Bains, A. *Woodwind Instruments and Their History*. New York, New York: W. W. Norton, 1963.

Carse, A. *Musical Wind Instruments*. New York, New York: Da Capo, 1965.

Cooper, L. *How Is Your Bassoon?* Royal Oaks, Michigan: Custom Music, 1974.

Donington, R. *Music and Its Instruments*. New York, New York: Methuen, 1982.

N.A.M.I.T. "Oboe/English Horn." *National Association of Musical Instrument Technicians*. South Bend, Indiana: NAMIT Publications, 1977.

Sadie, S. *The New Groves Dictionary of Musical Instruments*, Volume I. New York, New York: Groves, 1984.

Scribner, G. *The Scribner Guide to Orchestral Instruments*. New York, New York: C. Scribner, 1983.

Selmer. *Double Reeds*, Elkhart, Indiana: Selmer Division of the Magnavox Company, 1975.

Spencer, W. *The Art of Playing the Bassoon*. Evanston, Illinois: Summy-Birchard, 1969.

Stauffer, D. *Deficiencies of Wind Instruments in Ensembles*, Washington, DC: The Catholic University Press, 1954.

Stewart, A. *The Music Lover's Guide to the Instruments of the Orchestra*. New York, New York: Van Nostrand Reinhold, 1980.

CHAPTER EIGHT

BRASS INSTRUMENTS

In the section dealing with woodwind instruments, a separate chapter was devoted to each instrument because, in spite of the fact that the instruments are all categorized as woodwinds, they each have many characteristics which are unique. Brass instruments, on the other hand, tend to be alike in their acoustical and structural designs. Their sound generators, the mechanisms used to control their fundamental pitches, their acoustical idiosyncrasies, the materials used for construction, and their overall structures are all very similar. For this reason the chapter dealing with brass instruments focuses on the general attributes of the instruments, and then refers to the individual instrument's relationships to those attributes.

Brass instruments all produce sound by the player's buzzing his lips into a cup-shaped mouthpiece. With the exception of the trombone (and a few ancient and experimental instruments not commonly in use), all brass instruments alter their fundamental pitches by using *piston* or *rotary valves*. These valves open additional lengths of tubing to the vibrating column of air in the instrument, increasing, in effect, the length of the instrument and lowering the pitch. The *trombone* achieves the same result by using a *tubular slide* to extend the instrument's vibrating column.

Among the brass instruments currently in use are families of trumpets, trombones, French horns, tenor and baritone horns, and tubas. Each of these families is made up of an assortment of instruments of a similar design and size with variations primarily in the range, transposition or fundamental, and timbre. Presently, manufacturers produce a large assortment of trumpets, flugelhorns, cornets, trombones, alto horns, mellophones, tenor horns, euphoniums, baritone horns, tubas and sousaphones. These instruments are produced in different grades or models so that the variety is almost endless. Figure 8.1 shows just a few of the vast variety of brass instruments being offered at this time. Considering that each manufacturer makes modifications and additional models of the instruments, the potential number of different brass instruments available is mind boggling.

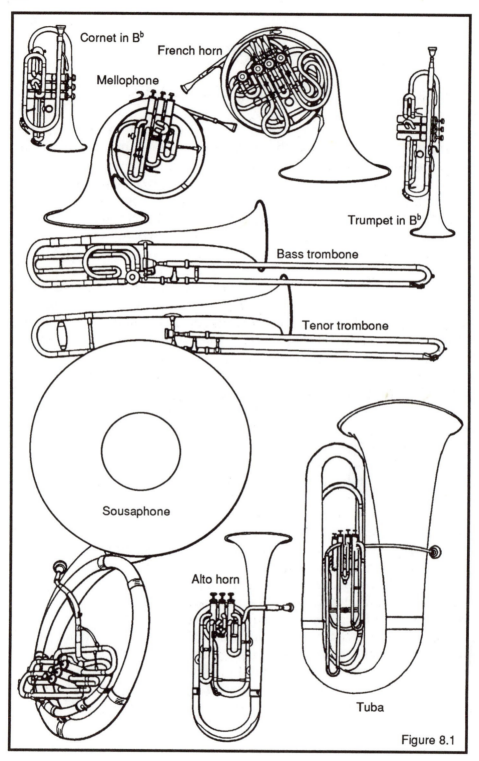

Cornet in B♭

French horn

Mellophone

Trumpet in B♭

Bass trombone

Tenor trombone

Sousaphone

Alto horn

Tuba

Figure 8.1

SOUND GENERATION

The sound generating process for all brass instruments begins with the human embouchure. As previously mentioned, the vibration or *buzzing of the lips* is the primary source of sound. The buzzing is directed into a *cup-shaped mouthpiece* that acts as a control or stabilizer for the vibration of the lips. This principle is often referred to as the *lip-reed principle*, because the lips are functioning as do the reeds in woodwind instruments. In implementing the lip-reed procedure, the upper lip is the source of vibration while the lower lip acts as the support for controlling the size of the aperture through which the air stream flows and enters the mouthpiece.

Since musicians cannot ordinarily control the size, shape, and structure of their embouchure, they must resort to developing control over the second step of the sound generating process, namely the mouthpiece. The *brass mouthpiece* consists of seven parts. Figure 8.2 shows a cross section of a trumpet mouthpiece. The parts shown are the rim, cup, shoulder, throat, backbore, and shank.

All brass mouthpieces have these components. The factor that distinguishes the mouthpieces for the different instruments is the size of their components and, therefore, the overall size of the mouthpiece. A tuba mouthpiece is much larger in all its dimensions than a trumpet mouthpiece. The design of the tuba mouthpiece is similar to all other brass mouthpieces, but it is sized to fill the acoustical requirements of the instrument.

The effectiveness of a mouthpiece is the result of the combination of its components in conjunction with the player's lip or embouchure. The totality of these factors ultimately becomes the sound generator. (The Vincent Bach Mouthpiece Manufacturing Company currently offers 268 possible combinations of mouthpiece components.)

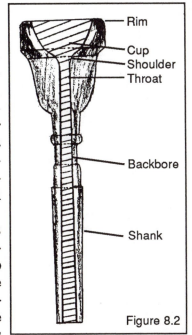

Figure 8.2

The *rim* of the mouthpiece is the part that comes into contact with the player's lips. The size and shape of the rim are generally described as being wide, narrow, round, or sharp (fig. 8.3). When selecting a mouthpiece, the first consideration must be the shape of the rim in relation to the player's embouchure. Since the rim size and shape profoundly affect the player's tone quality and endurance, it is important that the player select a rim which is best suited to his lip shape and size. The most effective width of the rim is usually similar to the lip size. Most players will need a medium rim. Players with thick lips would most likely benefit from using a wide rim, while players with thin lips should use a narrow rim. Although a reasonable degree of comfort is desirable, priority must be given to the sound generation response that the player will derive from the rim selected. The size and shape of the rim which produces the best sound, not the one that feels best, should be the one chosen.

The Selmer catalog of brass instrument mouthpieces includes a comprehensive description of mouthpieces available and a description of each size. (See the Selmer insert later on in this chapter.)

In the structure of the mouthpiece, the rim is followed by the *cup* (fig. 8.3). The factors to consider in choosing the cup are its

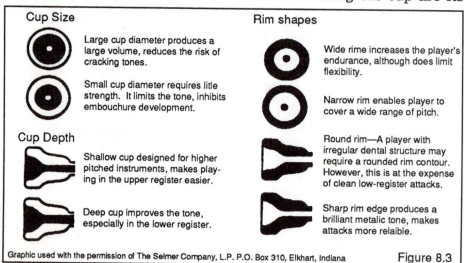

Cup Size

Large cup diameter produces a large volume, reduces the risk of cracking tones.

Small cup diameter requires litle strength. It limits the tone, inhibits embouchure development.

Cup Depth

Shallow cup designed for higher pitched instruments, makes playing in the upper register easier.

Deep cup improves the tone, especially in the lower register.

Rim shapes

Wide rime increases the player's endurance, although does limit flexibility.

Narrow rim enables player to cover a wide range of pitch.

Round rim—A player with irregular dental structure may require a rounded rim contour. However, this is at the expense of clean low-register attacks.

Sharp rim edge produces a brilliant metalic tone, makes attacks more relaible.

Graphic used with the permission of The Selmer Company, L.P. P.O. Box 310, Elkhart, Indiana

Figure 8.3

diameter and depth. The diameter provides the area in which the player's lips vibrate, so a diameter that is too small might restrict the vibration. Using the widest diameter possible will allow the player's lips more vibrating space and thereby permit a fuller sound.

The depth of a cup follows the principle of acoustics which permeates all of musical instrument design. The larger the instrument, the deeper and more mellow the sound. Deeper cups favor lower sounds, whereas shallower cups favor higher sounds.

The *shoulder* of the mouthpiece is the door to the throat (fig. 8.2) The shoulder controls the flow of air into the throat and in so doing greatly affects the tone quality.

The *throat* of the mouthpiece (fig. 8.2) also follows the general acoustical principles of size-to-pitch relationship, i.e., larger instruments favor lower sounds and vice versa. It is therefore necessary for the player to choose a mouthpiece throat size that will best serve the other components selected for the mouthpiece in question. However, since the throat controls the air flow, too small a size will tend to smother or mute the extreme registers, while too large an opening will not provide sufficient control to result in the optimum tone.

The *backbore* (fig. 8.2) of the brass mouthpiece is the column that follows the throat. This portion of the mouthpiece is not generally considered in terms of size but rather in terms of its shape. It starts out at the throat at its (the backbore's) narrowest and then enlarges as it reaches the end of the shank. Again, larger spaces produce deeper and louder sounds, while narrower or smaller spaces restrict the flow of air, offering more resistance and favoring higher sounds.

The *shank* (fig. 8.2) of the mouthpiece is the portion that enters the mouthpipe of the instrument. It is essential that the shank make perfect contact with the inside of the mouthpipe in order to avoid a leak or space that would cause turbulence in the flow of the vibrating air column.

Another consideration in evaluating brass mouthpieces is the materials from which they are made and the effects those materials have on tone production and playing ease. At the present time sterling silver, German nickel silver, silver- or gold-plated brass, plastic, aluminum, and stainless steel are the materials in use. There are as many opinions about which is best as there are players, but sterling silver, silver plate and nickel plate are by far the most popular.

One additional option available in the selection of mouthpieces for brass instruments is the *detachable rim*. This is a rim that screws on and can be used with mouth-pieces of various components. With a screw-on rim a player can switch mouthpieces when doubling on an instrument other than the player's usual instrument and not have to adjust to a different rim. The screw-on rim also allows the player to switch to a lucite rim when playing outdoors in cold weather. This is particularly convenient, since the player can avoid using a metal rim which can freeze onto the lips.

The following general principles of brass mouthpiece construction may help in the mouthpiece selection process.

1. Each player has a unique dental and lip structure that create a unique embouchure. It follows that each player needs a unique mouthpiece in order to produce the best possible sound.

2. Each instrument must have a mouthpiece that matches the design dimensions of that particular instrument, especially in relation to the size of the instrument's bore.

3. The mouthpiece's inner dimensions are critical to its output and must be matched with the player's needs and the bore of the instrument.

4. Mouthpiece model numbers and letters indicate the size of the various parts of the mouthpiece. Low numbers indicate larger cup diameters. High numbers indicate smaller cup diameters. Models without letters following the numbers have medium-deep cups producing a full, rich, deep sound. 'A' cups are very deep; 'B' cups are medium; 'C', medium shallow; 'D', shallow; 'E', extremely shallow; and 'W' models have a wide cushion rim for thick, soft lips.

In selecting a mouthpiece it is necessary first to evaluate the player's physiological characteristics and the instrument's structural requirements, then to determine the level of proficiency of the player, and finally, the nature of the player's performance needs. Then, on the basis of this information, determine what combination of mouthpiece components will serve the player best. It is essential that the player try a number of mouthpieces that approximate the proportions that have been decided on as most appropriate. In the final analysis, the response of the mouthpiece to the player's embouchure should determine the choice.

The following pages (figs. 8.4–8.13) are photocopies of the *Bach Embouchure and Mouthpiece Manual*. These pages indicate all of the possible combinations of components offered by the Selmer Company for brass mouthpieces. The information is intended to serve as a guide for the reader. The list, although reasonably comprehensive, is not all inclusive. Many other designs are available from other manufacturers.

The number of possible combinations of mouthpiece components can be expressed mathematically as seven factorial (7!) since seven different parts can be combined. This means (multiplying 7 x 6 x 5 x 4 x 3 x 2 x 1) that there are 5,040 possible combinations of mouthpiece components. Good luck!

Model No. and Depth of Cup	Rim Shape	Description
1-C Medium shallow	Medium wide.	Extra large cup for players with a robust embouchure. Produces an enormous volume of tone.
1 Medium deep	Medium wide.	Extra large cup for players with a robust embouchure. Principally used by trumpet players in large symphony orchestras who alternate between B♭,C,and D trumpets. Produces an enormous volume of tone of brilliant timbre.
1¼-C Medium shallow	Medium wide.	Extra large cup diameter for powerful symphony, opera and solo trumpeters. Well suited for interchanging between B♭,C, and D trumpets. Crystal clear, brilliant, yet compact tone of great carrying power throughout its register.
1½-C Medium shallow	Medium wide rim, not too sharp, very comfortable	Produces a natural tone of scintillating beauty and large volume. Superb high and low register. For players with a well-trained embouchure playing 1st trumpet in symphony orchestra.
2 Medium deep	Medium wide rim, lowered toward the outside.	Very large cup, powerful Teutonic quality of tone. For players with a good embouchure.
2-C Medium deep	Medium wide rim, lowered toward the outside.	Very large cup, powerful, brilliant tone. For symphony players with a good embouchure. Recommended for B♭,C, and D trumpets.
2½-C Medium shallow	Medium wide rim, lowered toward the outside.	Large cup; brilliant, heroic, crisp C trumpet tone. For symphony players with strong, muscular lips. Used for B♭,C,and D trumpet in many large symphony orchestras.

Figure 8.4

Model No. and Depth of Cup	Rim Shape	Description
2¾-C Medium shallow	Medium wide rim, lowered toward the outside. Slightly narrower than No. 2½-C.	Large cup; bright, lively C trumpet tone. For players with a healthy, normal embouchure. Fine for symphony work on B♭,C, and D trumpet.
3 Medium deep	Medium wide.	Fairly large cup; full, rich tone. Excellent for large symphony orchestra.
3-C Medium shallow	Medium wide.	Similar in size and rim to the previous model but more brilliant tone. For players who must use a large mouthpiece but want an easier high register.
5-A Deep	Medium wide with rounded inside edge.	A fairly large mouthpiece with a full, mellow, old-fashioned cornet tone. Good for church and solo work.
5-B Medium	Medium wide, lowered toward the outside. Medium sharp edge.	A precise rim and a fairly large cup. The tone is vivid and full. Well suited for all-round work.
5-C Medium shallow	Medium wide, well rounded toward the inside and the outside.	An excellent rim for players who do not like a sharp edge. The tone is lively and rich. A fine mouthpiece for players with a good embouchure in symphony and theater work.
6 Medium deep	Medium wide, not too sharp.	This model has an improved rim shape. It produces a rich, clear tone of substantial body. Vincent Bach prefers this model.
6-B Medium	Medium wide, not too sharp. Feels very comfortable on the lips.	This model produces a beautiful, ringing tone and responds easily. Its medium large size gives the lips sufficient room to execute freely.
6-C Medium shallow	Medium wide, Not too sharp. Comfortable on the lips.	This model has a distinctive C trumpet cup. Its clear tone cuts through even in the largest bands and orchestras. Very fine for C trumpet.
7 Medium deep	Medium wide, lower toward the outside. Medium sharp inside edge with a perfect grip. A most comfortable "lay."	This popular model, used by artists all over the world, produces a colorful, liquid tone which is uniform over the entire scale. Most desirable for all-round work.

Figure 8.5

Model No. and Depth of Cup	Rim Shape	Description
7-A Deep	Medium wide, lowered toward the outside. Medium sharp inside edge.	Melodious, rich tone, extremely effective for song playing. Its sweet, old-fashioned cornet tone approaches the quality of a lyric soprano voice. An ideal mouthpiece for cornet solos.
7-B Medium	Medium wide, lowered toward the outside. Medium sharp inside edge with a perfect grip. A most comfortable "lay."	Embodies the same features as the No. 7 model but has a slightly livelier timbre. Although full in the low and middle registers, this mouthpiece responds very easily on high tones and is therefore well suited to orchestra work where an effective, all-round register is essential.
7-BW Medium	Slightly wider cushion rim lowered toward the outside. Medium sharp inside edge with a perfect grip. A most comfortable "lay."	Embodies the same features as the No. 7-B, the same lively timbre and register. Its slightly wider rim is suitable for players with slightly heavier lips. Very effective for all-round work.
7-C Medium shallow	Medium wide, lowered toward the outside. Medium sharp inside edge with a perfect grip. A most comfortable "lay." Rim similar to the No. 7	The 7-C mouthpiece is probably the most widely used model in the world. Its sparkling, brilliant tone, free of nasal twang, is preferred by beginners and advanced school musicians who desire to progress quickly, and by symphony artists who regularly interchange between B♭, C, and D trumpets. It is a mouthpiece you can buy without trying if you are not set on any other model.
7-CW Medium shallow	Slightly wider cushion rim gradually lowered toward the outside. Very comfortable rim.	The No. 7-C mouthpiece with a slightly wider rim, like the 7-BW. It is suitable for players with slightly bigger lips. Very practical for doing extremely strenuous work in dance orchestras or parades. Also found in some of the finest American symphony orchestras. An excellent all-round mouthpiece.
7-D Very shallow	Medium wide, lowered toward the outside, similar to the 7-C rim, giving a perfect grip and comfortable "lay."	This mouthpiece has a shallower cup than the 7-C, designed principally for D trumpet, but used successfully in dance orchestras where a snappy tone, great brilliance, and easy high register are required. An ideal mouthpiece for players specializing in the extreme high register, offering great endurance.

Figure 8.6

Model No. and Depth of Cup	Rim Shape	Description
7-DW Very shallow	Slightly wider rim than the 7-C; practically the same as 7-CW.	This mouthpiece has an extra shallow E♭ soprano trumpet (or cornet) cup. Excellent for D trumpet, modern dance music, and circus work, playing continually in the high register. The slightly wide rim is helpful to players who play with a little too much pressure.
7-E Extra shallow	Medium wide like the No. 7-C	This mouthpiece has an extra shallow E♭ soprano trumpet (or cornet) cup and produces a very crisp, sparkling tone in the extreme high register. Although not recommended for B♭ trumpet work, players who prefer extremely shallow mouthpieces get excellent results with this model.
7-EW Extra shallow	Slightly wider cushion rim than No. 7-E; otherwise rim is similar to 7-CW or 7-DW	The description of the 7-E mouthpiece also applies to the 7-EW. Suitable for players who are accustomed to playing with much pressure, doing extremely hard work in dance orchestra or parades, mostly in the high register.
8 Medium deep	Fairly wide rim with a slightly flatter surface and rounded inside edge.	This model has exactly the same beautiful, rich tone and cup as the No. 7 but has a slightly flatter rim. Players with protruding teeth find the No. 8 very comfortable.
8-B Medium	Fairly wide rim with a slightly flatter surface than No. 7-B and rounded inner edge.	A model whose features correspond to those of the No. 7-B, with a slightly flatter rim better suited to players with protruding teeth. The fresh, lively tone, characteristic of all B models, finds superb expression in this mouthpiece.
8-C Medium shallow	Fairly wide rim with a slightly flatter surface than No. 7-C, rounded inside edge.	An improved C cup gives a penetrating, bright tone, very effective for virtuoso playing. The slightly flatter rim is suitable for players with protruding teeth.
8½ Medium deep	Medium wide, Lowered toward the outside. Has medium sharp inside edge which assures a firm grip.	Another model with a full, round tone, the same as the No. 7 but slightly smaller in diameter. Players with a sensitive embouchure, women, and those whose work is very strenuous prefer this model.

Figure 8.7

Model No. and Depth of Cup	Rim Shape	Description
8½-A Deep	Medium wide with rounded inner edge.	A mouthpiece with a full, velvety tone, suitable for solo or cantilena playing, and also for church work.
8½-B Medium	Medium wide, lowered toward the outside. The medium sharp edge assures a firm grip.	This model corresponds in design to the 7-B but with a cup diameter just enough smaller to facilitate producing the high tones without sacrificing beauty of tone. This model will increase the endurance of those who have weak embouchures.
8½-C Medium shallow	Medium wide, rim, well rounded	An easy responding mouthpiece with the improved C cup. This is the mouthpiece for those who want to "take it easy." The tone is brilliant and clear throughout the entire register. Great flexibility.
8¾ Medium deep	Medium wide rim, not too sharp. Comfortable "lay."	An excellent mouthpiece for legitimate work. Produces a rich, lyric tone of great volume and Teutonic character. Very effective in symphonic work and opera, especially in Wagnerian or Tschaikovsky compositions.
8¾-C Medium shallow	Medium wide, slightly flat facing.	Similar to the famous 7-C mouthpiece, but with a fraction smaller cup diameter. Superb high register, clear, bright tone, extremely easy response which adds to your endurance. An excellent model for players with delicate embouchures who suffer from early fatigue. Women cornetists with thin lips prefer this mouthpiece.
9 Medium deep	Medium wide rim, lowered toward the outside.	Another model with the same style of cup and rim as the famous No. 7, but with smaller cup diameter than the No. 8½. Has the same superb singing tone of the No. 7. Designed for players with narrow lips who find the previous models too large.
9-A Deep	Medium wide rim, well rounded.	Produces the mellow, sweet cornet tone so popular in the times of Clarke, Levy, Arbuckle, Hoch, etc.
9-B Medium	Medium wide rim, lowered toward the outside.	Corresponds with the No. 9 but has a slightly livelier tone. Players with narrow lips who tire quickly feel relieved when using this model.

Figure 8.8

Model No. and Depth of Cup	Rim Shape	Description
9-C Medium shallow	Medium wide rim, lowered toward the outside.	Similar in size to the No. 9, but producing a more brilliant, open tone. Free high register, easy response. Suitable for strenuous all-round work by players with narrow lips who tire quickly.
9-D Very shallow	Medium wide rim, lowered toward the outside.	This model is similar in size to the No. 9 and in tone to the more brilliant No. 7 mouthpiece. Players with narrow, sensitive lips who tire quickly get satisfactory results with this model. Recommended for heavy work in the extreme high register and for use on D trumpets.
10 Medium deep	Fairly wide rim with a rather broad, flat surface.	A mouthpiece with a solid tone like the No. 7, but smaller in size and with a broad, flat rim. Suitable for players with fleshy, soft lips. Excellent for parade work.
10-B Medium	Fairly wide, similar to the No. 10 rim.	Same size as the No. 10 but with brighter, more metallic ringing tone. Will give good results to players with heavy, thick lips—especially those who become easily fatigued.
10-C Medium shallow	Fairly wide rim with a rather broad, flat surface.	Same rim as the No. 10, but with a shallow C cup. Especially designed for high notes and sparkling brilliancy. Its very easy blowing makes it a great boon to players whose lips need support.
10½-A Deep	Medium wide rim, well rounded.	This model has a mellow, rich, lyric cornet tone good for melody work. Favored by players of the Italian school.
10½-C Medium shallow	Medium wide comfortable rim.	This marvelous mouthpiece is an even contender with the No. 7-C as the most popular of all models. It has a remarkably fine high register, a rich, resonating low register, and offers great endurance. It is particularly useful to players without a strong embouchure or women. The ideal mouthpiece for solo work and for C trumpet.
10½-CW Medium shallow	Extra wide cushion rim, high toward the inner edge.	The size and cup shape are similar to the No. 10½-C and the playing qualities correspond to this model. Recommended for players who play with very heavy pressure, especially those with thick, fleshy lips. Well liked by dance musicians.

Figure 8.9

Model No. and Depth of Cup	Rim Shape	Description
10½-D Very shallow	Medium comfortable rim, similar to the 10½-C rim.	Similar in size to the No. 10½-C, with a shallower cup for more brilliancy and an easier high register. Principally used for modern dance orchestra work in the high register, especially by players with a rather weak embouchure. Excellent for high D trumpet and for soprano E♭ trumpet in oratorios.
10½-DW Very shallow	Extra wide cushion rim high toward the inner edge.	Same depth of cup and diameter as 10½-D, with an extra wide rim. Has the same brilliant, crisp tone as the 10½-D and is recommended to players with heavy, fleshy lips, especially if soft and not muscular. Good for high D and soprano E♭ trumpet.
10½-E Extra shallow	Medium wide comfortable rim	This model produces the same scintillating tone as the No. 7-E. It is given preference by players with weak lips who have to play much in the high register. Ideal for high E♭ soprano cornet or trumpet in high F.
10½-EW Extra shallow	Extra wide cushion rim, high toward the inner edge.	Cup diameter and cup shape are the same as the previous model No. 10½-E but the extra wide rim offers support to players who have soft, fleshy lips and play continually in the extreme high register. Good for tough dance work, for E♭ soprano trumpet or cornet, and for piccolo trumpet in high F.
10¾-A Deep	Medium wide rim, well rounded.	Slightly smaller cup diameter than the No. 10½-A. Also possesses a mellow, sweet tone. Good for melody playing. Generally used by players of the Italian school.
10¾-CW Medium shallow	Extra wide cushion rim.	This model is slightly smaller in cup diameter than the 10½-CW. For the "high note" artist who desires a very brilliant tone, and for players with thick, fleshy lips who are accustomed to using much pressure. There is no easier blowing mouthpiece with such voluminous tone as the No. 10¾-CW.
10¾-EW Extra shallow	Extra wide cushion rim.	Shallower than the 10¾-CW to produce a very penetrating, glittering tone. For extreme high register work, and for E♭ soprano cornet.

Figure 8.10

Model No. and Depth of Cup	Rim Shape	Description
11-A Deep	Medium wide rim, well rounded.	A small mouthpiece with a round, full, old-fashioned cornet tone. Suitable for melody playing or church work, especially for players who have little time to practice.
11-B Medium	Medium wide rim, well rounded.	A medium small mouthpiece with a beautiful, metallic, clear tone. Responds very easily, especially in the upper register. Players with delicate embouchures and women cornetists get highly satisfactory results with this model.
11-C Medium shallow	Medium wide, comfortable rim.	Similar to the No. 10½-C but slightly smaller. This mouthpiece has a beautiful, brilliant C trumpet tone. Requires little effort to play in the high register, yet produces a free low range. Players with sensitive embouchures can use this mouthpiece to great advantage.
11-D Very shallow	Medium wide, comfortable rim. Well rounded.	Cup diameter is the same as the No. 11-C but slightly shallower for D trumpet. Produces a still more brilliant tone. Very effective in the high register. Good for dance orchestra work, players not having a strong embouchure, and women cornetists.
11-DW Very shallow	Extra wide cushion rim.	Same cup as 11-D, with wider rim. Players with thick, fleshy lips, especially those who do not have sufficient basic training to rely on the strength of their lip muscles, can use this mouthpiece to advantage. Produces crisp easy top tones.
11-EW Extra shallow	Extra wide cushion rim, rather high toward the inner edge.	A mouthpiece especially designed for playing in the extreme high register. This model has the same cup diameter as the three previous models, but because of the extra shallow cup, the tone is very brilliant, piercing, and cuts very well through the rest of the orchestra. Used by players who specialize in very high register work, using heavier than normal pressure.
11½-A Deep	Medium wide rim, well rounded.	Similar to Model No. 11-A but slightly smaller. Produces a rich, round tone. Designed for song playing and church work.

Figure 8.11

Model No. and Depth of Cup	Rim Shape	Description
11½-C Medium shallow	Comfortable, medium wide rim.	Similar to the No. 10½-C, with slightly smaller cup diameter. An excellent mouthpiece with a brilliant, scintillating tone, very easy response and good, all-round register. Recommended to young girls who are not physically strong.
11¾-C Medium shallow	Medium wide, well rounded.	The style of this mouthpiece is similar to the No. 11½-C (corresponding also to the No. 7-C and No. 10-C). It is slightly smaller than the previous model, easy playing, with a compact, brilliant tone. Recommended for a weak, sensitive embouchure and for young girls, especially those with narrow lips.
11¾-CW Extra shallow	Fairly wide, rather flat cushion rim. Not too sharp.	The cup diameter is similar to the No. 10¾-A. Used by players with soft, fleshy lips who rely on more pressure than the average player. Responds easily in the high register.
12 Medium deep	Broad, rather flat rim.	This popular model produces a full, mellow tone. Players of the English or Italian school who are accustomed to small mouthpieces choose this model. A good choice for players with heavy, weak lips.
12-B Medium	Broad, rather flat rim.	This model has the same rim as the No. 12, with a slighly shallower cup to make the tone more lively and bright. The high register responds with ease. Best suited for players with heavy, soft lips.
12-C Medium shallow	Broad, rather flat rim.	This model's brilliant, snappy tone is just the thing for trumpeters who have to play forte in the upper range and for long hours. Players with heavy, weak lips who have difficulty with the high tones obtain excellent results with it.
12-CW Medium shallow	Broad, rather flat rim. Extra wide cushion rim, high toward the inside.	Cup diameter and depth of cup are the same as the No. 12-C mouthpiece, but the extra wide rim makes this model suitable for players with very heavy, weak lips who rely on using pressure for producing the high tones.
17 Medium deep	Medium wide rim.	A small mouthpiece with a solid, compact tone. Players with thin lips find this model highly satisfactory.

Figure 8.12

Model No. and Depth of Cup	Rim Shape	Description
17-C Medium shallow	Medium wide rim.	This small mouthpiece has a lively, clear and brilliant tone. For players with thin lips whose embouchure becomes easily fatigued.
18 Medium deep	Broad, rather flat rim.	Has the same cup and size as the No. 17 but a wider rim. Players of the old Italian or English school having heavy, soft lips and a rather sensitive embouchure choose this model.
18-C Medium shallow	Broad, rather flat rim.	Same cup diameter and shape as the No. 17-C. The wider and flatter rim distributes the pressure over a larger surface to prevent cutting off the blood circulation.
20-C Medium shallow	Medium wide rim.	A very small mouthpiece, recommended only to players who have extremely weak or delicate lips or have used a very small mouthpiece during their entire musical career. It helps players who have difficulty playing above the middle register.

Figure 8.13

AMPLIFICATION

The sound generated by the mouthpiece of any brass instrument sets into motion the column of air that is present in the instrument. The flow of air from the player's lips does not travel through the instrument and come out of the bell end. In fact practically nothing comes out of the bell end of the instrument except the sound. The function of the breath is to set the lips of the performer into vibration. That vibration is transmitted to the air column contained within the tubing of the instrument. When that air column is set into motion, sound is heard. The sound is then altered by the player's lengthening or shortening the tubing by one of several mechanical means to be discussed later in the section called *Mechanisms*.

An experiment conducted by William Thieck ("Common Sense Lip and Tone Development," 1928) consisted of rarefying the air in a trumpet by pouring gasoline into the instrument before playing. The result was no sound in spite of the proper sound generation procedure followed by the player, because there was no air present in the trumpet to vibrate. Another experiment by O. A. Peterson ("The Cornet," 1924) consisted of diverting the air flow produced by the player's buzzing lips before that air could reach the lead pipe and enter the body of the instrument. He accomplished this by placing a thin membrane in the shank of the mouthpiece and drilling a small hole at the top of the mouthpiece in order to allow the player's breath to escape immediately after causing the buzz. The result was sound emitting from the instrument because there was a column of air in the instrument to vibrate.

When a player initiates a buzz into a BB♭ tuba, a sound occurs immediately in spite of the fact that the player's breath does not have time to travel throughout the entire instrument to produce that sound. It would take several full breaths to fill up the tubing of the instrument before any air could reach the bell. The sound is caused by the buzzing of the players lip's exciting the existing air in the instrument.

Tone produced on a musical instrument contains not only one pitch but a *fundamental* pitch plus a series of sounds called *upper partials* or *overtones* (see chapter one, p. 2). The natural order of upper partials contains an inherent problem of diminishing interval relationship. The higher the interval in the harmonic structure, the closer the tonal relationship of the two notes creating the interval. Brass instruments' use of the upper partials increases in number as the instrument rises in its relationship to its family members. (A tuba utilizes open tones that are further apart from each other than those of the French horn.) This being the case, a problem of inconsistency of intonation arises which is inherent in all brass instruments. The intervals which occur higher up on the overtone series will be smaller in size by a small fraction than the same interval taken from a lower point in the overtone series (fig. 8.14). Therefore, a minor third between the sixth and seventh partials, e.g. G-B♭, would be smaller than one between the fifth and six partials, E-G. Since most tones

played on brass instruments are harmonics, they are, by their very nature, not true in pitch and so the brass players' problems begin.

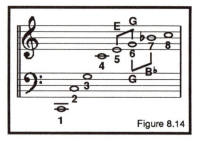

Figure 8.14

The bore of brass instruments is often a subject of great confusion, disagreement, and misinterpretation. It is often said, for example, that the trumpet has a cylindrical bore while the cornet has a conical bore. In fact neither is entirely the case. Brass instruments use a combination of conical- and cylindrical-shaped tubing to form the body and mechanism of the instruments. The mouthpipe, valve, and bell section of brass instruments each require a different shape and size in order to function in a prescribed manner (fig. 8.15). The changing of the bore size of any one of these sections will change the quality of the sound produced.

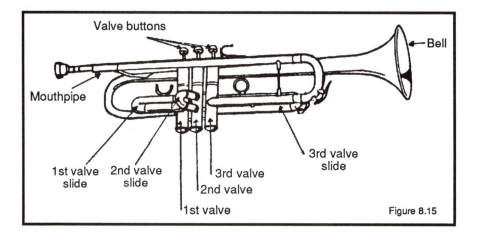

Figure 8.15

Most often, bore sizes of brass instruments are referred to as being either large, medium, or small. There is no industry standard for the exact dimensions of these categories and so, when the terms are used, the interpretation of their meanings must be judged in a broad sense. It is generally accepted that the larger the bore size, the deeper the sound. Large-bore instruments produce a Teutonic sound, medium bores permit more flexibility for the player, and small bores produce a brighter, crisper sound.

When a sound is produced on brass instruments, the natural sequence of the overtone series occurs. In order to produce each of the seven fundamentals and all of their respective upper partials, the body of the instrument must be a different length for each fundamental. In order to achieve this, the design of the instrument must in some way facilitate the availability of seven different lengths of tubing for the player to utilize at will. This is accomplished by a system of valves that open ports leading to additional tubing or by a slide, such as is found on a slide trombone, which lengthens the instrument's vibrating column.

MECHANISMS

Unlike the woodwind instruments' key systems, the mechanisms used to manipulate the sounds generated on brass instruments are not at all complicated or intimidating in appearance. The mechanical principle utilized extends the size of the instrument by the player's either activating a *piston* or *rotary valve*, or extending a slide. This allows more tubing to be available for the vibrating air column, thereby lowering the pitch.

The slide used on the trombone is the simplest of systems and the most reliable in providing the performer with the opportunity to produce accurate intonation. Since the player is able to locate the slide anywhere within its range, complete control of the length of the vibrating column is available and, therefore, complete control of intonation. The slide trombone offers the best opportunity for playing a brass instrument in tune (fig. 8.16).

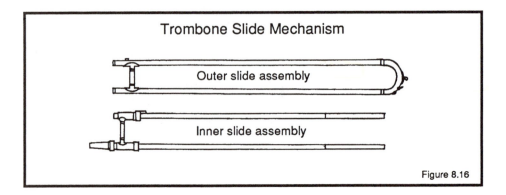

Trombone Slide Mechanism

Outer slide assembly

Inner slide assembly

Figure 8.16

Valves, on the other hand, restrict the player in that they can only be fully depressed or fully released with no options in between. The result is a myriad of intonation complications which are virtually insurmountable. When the player depresses a piston valve, the holes in the piston are realigned, extending the length of the valve slide associated with that valve (fig. 8.17). The rotary valve serves the same function as the piston, but instead of traveling up and down like the piston, the rotary valve turns in its casing. When the valve rotates, it realigns its ports to open up new valve slide sections, increasing the length of the vibrating column of air and lowering the pitch (fig. 8.18). Rotary valves are most commonly used on French horns, less commonly on tubas and trumpets.

Although both types of valves effect the same result, they differ in their response. Piston type valves permit better articulation and must be depressed by the player without any sideward pressure in order to be effective. Failure to depress the piston valve in a true vertical direction will result in its scraping on the interior wall of the valve casing. This will decrease the effective accuracy of the piston. Rotary valves, when functioning properly, are considered by many to be easier to use, allowing the player greater agility.

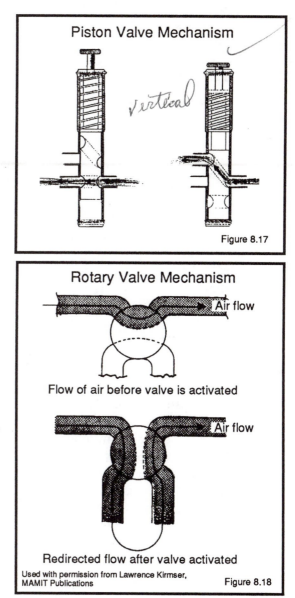

Piston Valve Mechanism

vertical

Figure 8.17

Rotary Valve Mechanism

Air flow

Flow of air before valve is activated

Air flow

Redirected flow after valve activated

Used with permission from Lawrence Kirmser, MAMIT Publications

Figure 8.18

Inherent in the design of trumpets using the rotary valve design is the placement of the first valve about two inches from the mouthpipe instead of the usual ten inches as on a piston-valve design. This structural difference results in a less accurate scale in pitch production along with some loss of brilliance.

On all brass instruments, the valves, regardless of type or design, serve the same function. The first valve lowers the fundamental tone being produced by the player by one full step. The second valve lowers the fundamental by one half-step and the third valve lowers the fundamental by one-and-one-half steps (fig. 8.19). The

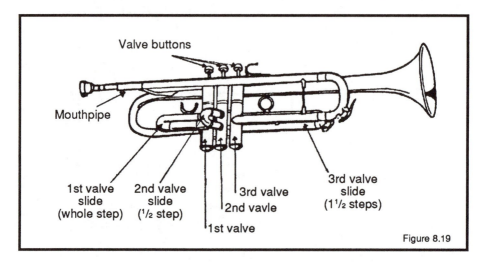

Figure 8.19

theory is quite simple to understand. Unfortunately, these simple mechanical processes create a potpourri of acoustical complications which have to date remained the nemesis of the brass player.

Intonation difficulties occur because occidental (Western) music uses the tempered scale intended for keyboard instruments, whereas brass instruments are built to produce the natural or 'just' scale—the result of the natural harmonic series of overtones. As these two scales approach their extreme ranges, the comparative frequencies differ, so that open G5 on the trumpet produces a pitch which is higher than that of the same note on the tempered scale.

An even greater problem of intonation arises when the valve systems are activated. Recall that the second valve lowers the fundamental by one half-step, the first valve by two half-steps and the third valve by three half-steps. When the second valve is depressed on a trumpet, the instrument is converted from its natural B^b overtone series to an A-overtone series. This, creates, in effect a new instrument, a trumpet in A instead of in B^b. A trumpet in A is longer than a trumpet in B^b and, therefore, requires longer tubing for the first and third slides, if the ratio of these slides is to remain consistent with the new length of the instrument. Of course the first and third slides do not change and so, when additional valves are activated in conjunction with the second slide, intonation begins to fail. There are two problems—that of the just, as opposed to the tempered scale, and that of the distorted ratios incurred by the use of the valves. They may be compensated for but not totally corrected by the manufacturer's selecting a mid-point in the length of the valve slides to ease the problem of pitch and provide the least possible inaccuracy of pitch under all conditions. In addition to that compromise, many brass instruments are fitted with valve slide mechanisms allowing the player to quickly and easily adjust the length of the particular slide in use at that moment.

As stated at the beginning of this chapter, the mechanics of valve instruments are not particularly complex. Simply, a piston, a rotor, or a slide does the job. Unfortunately, two of these three systems, namely, the rotor and the piston, do not offer the performer an opportunity to play his instrument in perfect tune, but instead create problems of intonation which do not exist on the original brass instruments before valves are added. On the other hand, without valves one is limited to the overtone series as performed by embouchure changes. It is obvious that the addition of valves is the lesser of the two evils.

THE BRASS FAMILY

Brass instruments have been in existence for centuries in one form or another. A large variety of the instruments are still in use and an even larger variety are currently being produced and sold for contemporary performing groups. Brass instrument names often contain three terms that describe the kind of instrument, its practical performance range, and the overtone series upon which its acoustical design is based. An example would be the soprano trumpet in B♭, a (1) trumpet which plays in the (2) soprano range with a fundamental overtone series, i.e. without the use of valves, in (3) B♭.

Below is an annotated list of the more common contemporary brass instruments.

TRUMPET: (fig. 8.20) The trumpet's effective sound producing and amplification system begins with a cup shaped mouthpiece usually made of brass, coated with silver. The mouthpiece is inserted into a slightly conical-shaped tube called a mouthpiece receiver, which in turn is connected to the main body of the instrument. The major portion of the trumpet is cylindrical and contains the cylinders that house the valves. The valves can be either of the piston or rotary type.

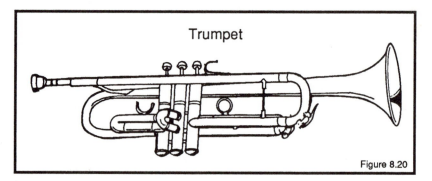

Trumpet

Figure 8.20

Following the main cylindrical section of the instrument is the bell section. This is again conical in shape and is about one quarter the length of the preceding cylinder.

The trumpet is designed with a tuning slide for each valve. At present the following list of trumpets is being manufactured and used most commonly: mezzo-soprano in C and B♭, soprano in D, high E♭, high F, sopranino in high G, piccolo in high B♭, contralto in low E♭ and F, and tenor in C and B♭.

CORNET: (fig. 8.21) While the trumpet is primarily cylindrical with some conical parts, the cornet is almost totally conical. Sharing essentially the same design principles as the trumpet, the cornet begins with a cup-shaped mouthpiece somewhat smaller than that of the trumpet. This is connected to a lead pipe which joins the remainder of the body of the instrument. The overall instrument is shorter than the trumpet because the tubing is usually bent into two loops. The combination of the smaller conical bore and the two turns

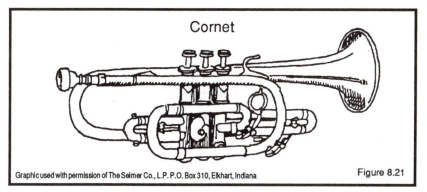

Cornet

Graphic used with permission of The Selmer Co., L.P. P.O. Box 310, Elkhart, Indiana

Figure 8.21

in the tubing present greater resistance to the player with the resulting tone being mellower than that of the trumpet. Currently in use are the mezzo-soprano cornet in B♭ and soprano in high E♭.

FLUGELHORN: (fig. 8.22) This instrument is, in effect, a bass trumpet. It has the same range and pitch as the trumpet but demonstrates its unique characteristics in the contralto range, where it produces a tone which has a rich, mellow timbre. The instrument is available in mezzo-soprano in B♭ and bass in B♭.

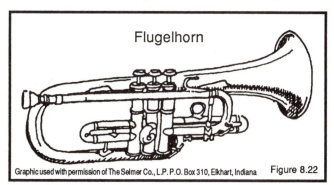

Flugelhorn

Graphic used with permission of The Selmer Co., L.P. P.O. Box 310, Elkhart, Indiana

Figure 8.22

FRENCH HORN: (fig. 8.23) French horns are manufactured in B♭, F, and a combination of the B♭ and F horns, called a double horn. Using a double horn, the player can switch from B♭ to F by pressing a thumb trigger, which turns a rotary valve to redirect the vibrating column of air from one section of tubing to another. Switching from F to B♭ enables the player to avoid playing the high notes which depend on upper partials of the overtone series. Due to their close interval proximity, these notes present difficulties in tone placement.

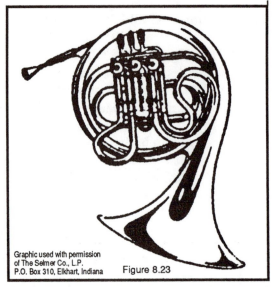

Graphic used with permission of The Selmer Co., L.P. P.O. Box 310, Elkhart, Indiana

Figure 8.23

The (single) French horn in F manufactured today consists of a coiled tube about 76 inches long. The addition of the B♭ crook increases the length by 52½ inches. The total length of the combined F-B♭ (double) horn becomes 11 feet 8½ inches. The single horn in F contains three rotary valves which open and close the various lengths of tubing. A fourth valve is used when the B♭ crook is added to the single horn to make a double F-B♭ instrument. The bore of the instrument is conical up to and including the bell, which ends in a diameter of about 12 inches.

The three horns currently in use are the horns in F, B♭, and the double (F and B♭ combined).

MELLOPHONE: (fig. 8.24) The mellophone resembles a French horn and is used as a substitute for the horn when an actual French horn is not practical or available. The instrument is played with piston valves located for use with the right hand. The mellophone is useful when quick

Graphic used with permission of The Selmer Co., L.P. P.O. Box 310, Elkhart, Indiana

Plate LXIX

from the trumpet or cornet to a French horn-like instrument are required. Mellophones are available in E♭ and F.

TROMBONE: (fig. 8.25) The slide trombone is the only brass instrument that can be played in tune. This is so because instead of valves, the trombone uses a slide to lengthen or shorten the amplifier or bore of the instrument. If the player is capable of discerning proper pitch placement, there is no limit to the level of pitch perfection

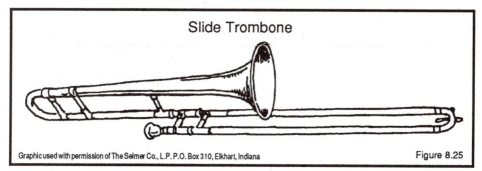

Slide Trombone

Graphic used with permission of The Selmer Co., L.P. P.O. Box 310, Elkhart, Indiana   Figure 8.25

attainable since the slide can be placed at any point necessary to achieve accurate intonation.

Due to the slide design, the bore of the instrument must be primarily cylindrical. The exception occurs with the taper of the bell section which flares out to about eight to nine inches at the widest point. This section of the instrument is equal to about one-third of the entire length of the instrument.

Trombones come in an assortment of models, among which are the alto in E♭, tenor in B♭, symphony in B♭, bass in B♭, valve in B♭, and trombonium in B♭.

VALVE TROMBONE: (fig. 8.26) This instrument has the appearance of a trombone except that there are three piston valves incorporated into the slide design and the slide portion is stationary. The primary use of the valve trombone is to facilitate a lower brass player in doubling on the trombone.

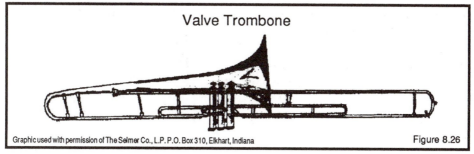

Valve Trombone

Graphic used with permission of The Selmer Co., L.P. P.O. Box 310, Elkhart, Indiana   Figure 8.26

ALTO HORN: (fig. 8.27) The upright E♭ alto horn is primarily a marching instrument and is often used in place of the French horn. Easy to carry, this instrument has a brassy tone and is predominantly used as a support to the rhythm section of the marching band. The alto horn is made in E♭ only.

Alto Horn

Graphic used with permission
of The Selmer Co., L.P.
P.O. Box 310, Elkhart, Indiana   Figure 8.27

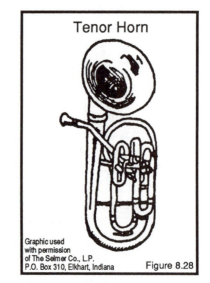

Tenor Horn

Graphic used
with permission
of The Selmer Co., L.P.
P.O. Box 310, Elkhart, Indiana   Figure 8.28

TENOR HORN: (fig. 8.28) More commonly used in central Europe, the tenor horn, so named for its range placement in the scheme of brass instruments, is used for solo passages that require more virtuosity than those normally associated with instruments in the lower range. The tenor horn is built in the key of B♭.

BARITONE HORN: (fig. 8.29) Representing the baritone voice in the brass family, the instrument is less versatile than the B♭ tenor horn and has a more mellow voice. The baritone horn is used most often in American concert bands and is built on the B♭ overtone series.

Baritone Horn

Graphic used
with permission
of The Selmer Co., L.P.
P.O. Box 310, Elkhart, Indiana   Figure 8.29

EUPHONIUM: (fig. 8.30) A form of tenor or baritone horn producing a rich mellow tone because of its large bell bore, the euphonium is best left to perform slow lyrical bass solos. Like the baritone, it too is built on the B^b overtone series.

TUBA: (fig. 8.31) The tuba, lowest of the brass instruments, comes in several designs. The upright bell is used primarily for concert work, while the recording model, or bell front model, is used for marching. In addition there is the famous tuba designed for marching known as the sousaphone (fig. 8.32). Tubas are built with three and four valves in either piston or rotary design. The various models available are the rotary valve in BB^b and CC, three valve in BB^b and E^b, four valve in BB^b, and sousaphone in BB^b and E^b.

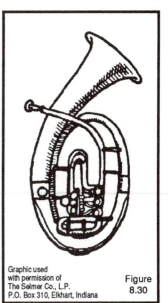

Graphic used
with permission of
The Selmer Co., L.P.
P.O. Box 310, Elkhart, Indiana

Figure 8.30

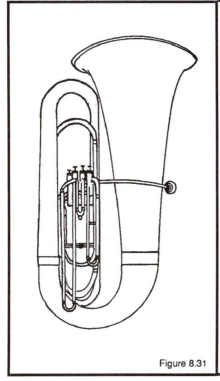

Figure 8.31

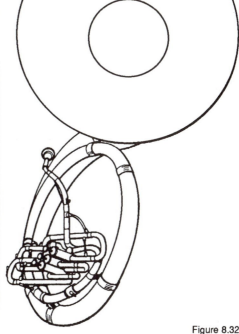

Figure 8.32

This overview describes only some of the vast assortments of brass instruments that are currently on the market and in use. There also exists a complete line of brass instruments called *marching brass*. Marching brass instruments are identical to the above in function, except that they are designed to be held in a horizontal playing position, as one would hold a trumpet in order to facilitate playing while marching.

SUMMARY

The manner in which brass instruments function acoustically, mechanically, and musically is almost identical. The materials from which they are made are the same. They all use a lip reed with a cup mouthpiece coupled with a brass amplifying system fitted with valves which extend the length of the amplifier. (The slide trombone is the exception). Unfortunately, this family of instruments also shares the characteristic (again with the exception of the slide trombone) of having inherent intonation problems.

The problems begin with the sound generator being the human lips functioning as a reed or buzzing device. Through this system of sound generation, the brass player is restricted to the limitations inherent in his or her own lip and mouth configuration. The brass player does not have the option of changing the components of the tone generator as do other instrumentalists. Single reed players can change mouth-pieces, reeds, and ligatures. Double reed players have their reeds made to order or make them themselves. String players (as will be explained in the following chapter) have a vast variety of strings, bows and bridge configurations at their disposal.

Whereas all other instrumentalists can select components with which they can customize their sound generators, brass players are born with theirs. The only outside assistance they can turn to is the cup mouthpiece. There are numerous mouthpiece designs available to accommodate the infinite number of shapes of lip-mouth configurations. Ultimately, however, brass players, unlike other instrumentalists, simply cannot change their reeds.

The second problem that is unique to brass instruments, (again with the exception of the slide trombone), is that of the change in valve-slide ratios as the pistons are depressed. Devices such as the valve slide trigger and the addition of a fourth valve on some instruments, along with some creative concepts in bore construction, all have helped to improve the intonation problems. However, it is apparent that the valve system used on brass instruments at best provides an inexact system of intonation. Listeners have adjusted to these imperfect sounds by sheer exposure, tending to accept the sound of the brass section as being a product of timbre rather than of imperfect intonation. In fact, we have become accustomed to it and consequently find it acceptable. Of all the problems with instruments in use at this time, the brass player's plight is the most difficult in the area of intonation. Good intonation on a brass instrument must rest with the ability of the performer to humor individual notes as required by each situation.

The brass choir provides the power and brilliance essential to the performance of orchestral music, as it evolved with the works of Beethoven, Brahms, and Wagner during the Romantic period. Military, ceremonial, and entertainment bands could not fill their roles without the brass choir's dynamic character. So, as is the case with anything we love and need, we accept it for its virtues and live with its imperfections.

Below and on the following pages are photocopies from the repair parts catalog of United Musical Instruments U.S.A., Inc., Elkhart, Indiana. These pages show breakdowns of common brass instruments, indicating the parts of the body and key mechanism.

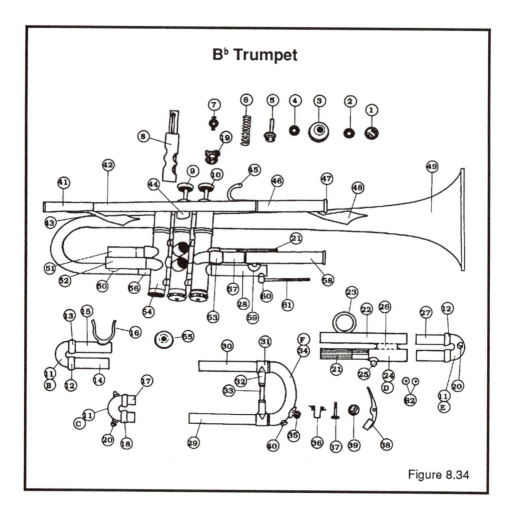

Figure 8.34

B♭ Trumpet — Key to Parts

ITEM NO.	NOMENCLATURE	ITEM NO.	NOMENCLATURE
1	Finger button	35	Water key bridge
2	Finger button felt - black/white	36	Water key spring
3	Top cap	37	Water key screw
4	Piston stem felt - black	38	Water key
5	Piston stem	39	Water key cork
6	Piston spring	40	Water key nipple
7	Piston guide	41	Receiver
8	#1 piston	42	Mouthpipe
9	#2 piston	43	Brace - receiver/bell
10	#3 piston	44	Ballister brace - leadpipe
11	Slide crook	45	Finger hook
12	Slide ferrule, lower	46	Outside tube - upper
13	Slide ferrule, upper	47	Bead ring
14	Inside lower 1st slide	48	Brace - tuning slide/bell
15	Outside upper 1st slide	49	Bell (2X)
16	Thumb hook	50	Brace - 1st/bell
17	Inside 2nd slide	51	Inside tube - upper
18	2nd slide ferrule	52	Outside tube - lower
19	Ballister brace assembly - bell	53	Ferrule
20	Pull knob	54	Valve assembly
21	Inside tube - long	55	Botton cap
22	Outside tube - long	56	Ferrule
23	Finger ring	57	Extension tube - tuning slide
24	Outside tube - short	58	Outside tube - lower
25	Stop post - large hole	59	Brace - 3rd/tuning slide
26	Brace bar	60	Stop post - threaded hole
27	Inside tube - short	61	Stop rod
28	Outside slide tube	62	Slide stop nut
29	Inside tube - long	A	Piston assembly (complete)
30	Inside tube - short	B	#1 slide assembly
31	Ferrule	C	#2 slide assembly
32	Brace socket	D	#3 slide assembly (center assy.)
33	Brace rod	E	#3 slide assembly (end assy.)
34	Crook	F	Main slide assembly

Key to Figure 8.34

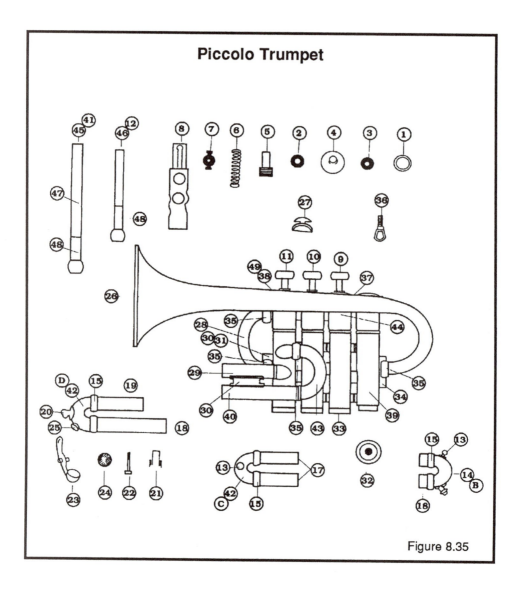

Figure 8.35

Piccolo Trumpet — Key to Parts

ITEM NO.	NOMENCLATURE
1	Finger button
2	Piston stem felt - black
3	Felt-black/white
4	Top cap
5	Piston stem
6	Piston spring
7	Piston guide
8	#1 piston
9	#2 piston
10	#3 piston
11	#4 piston
12	"B^b" trumpet mouthpipe tuner
13	Pull knob
14	Slide crook - 1st slide
15	Slide ferrule
16	Inside 1st slide
17	Inside 3rd slide
18	Inside lower 4th slide
19	Inside upper 4th slide
20	Water key bridge
21	Water key spring
22	Water key screw
23	Water key lever
24	Water key cork
25	Water key nipple
26	Piccolo trumpet bell
27	Ballister brace - leadpipe
28	Mouthpipe return crook
29	Outside upper 4th slide
30	Slide brace bar
31	Outside 3rd slide
32	Bottom cap
33	Crook cap (2nd slide)
34	Outside 1st slide
35	Connecting ferrule
36	Thumbscrew
37	Split nut
38	Mouthpipe receiver tube
39	Valve assembly
40	Lower outside 4th slide
41	"A" trumpet mouthpipe tuner
42	Slide crook - 3rd & 4th slide
43	Crook - large 4th slide
44	Ballister brace - bell
45	"A" mouthpipe
46	"B^b" mouthpipe
47	Mouthpipe extension tube
48	Receiver
49	Outside mouthpipe assembly
A	Piston assembly
B	1st slide assembly
C	3rd slide assembly
D	4th slide assembly

Key to Figure 8.35

100

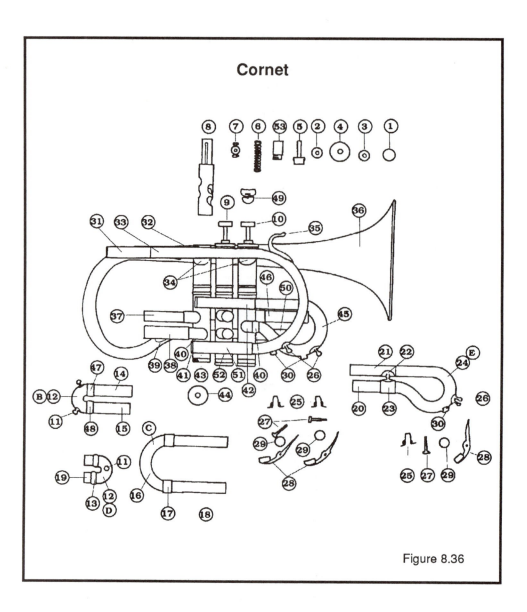

Cornet

Figure 8.36

Cornet — Key to Parts

ITEM NO.	NOMENCLATURE
1	Finger button
2	Piston stem felt - black
3	Felt-black/white
4	Top cap
5	Piston stem
6	Piston spring
7	Piston guide
8	#1 piston
9	#2 piston
10	#3 piston
11	Pull knob
12	Slide crook
13	2nd slide ferrule
14	Outside upper 1st slide
15	Inside lower 1st slide
16	Tuning slide crook
17	Tuning slide ferrule
18	Inside tuning slide tube
19	Inside 2nd slide tube
20	Inside lower 3rd slide
21	Outside upper 3rd slide
22	Slide brace assembly
23	3rd slide ferrule
24	3rd slide crook
25	Water key spring
26	Water key bridge
27	Water key screw
28	Water key lever
29	Water key cork
30	Water key nipple
31	Mouthpiece receiver
32	Bell/receiver brace
33	Mouthpipe tube
34	Ballister brace - leadpipe
35	Finger hook
36	Cornet bell
37	Inside upper 1st slide
38	Outside lower 1st slide
39	Bell/slide brace
40	Bell connecting ferrule
41	Bead ring
42	Outer tuning slide - upper
43	Valve assembly
44	Bottom cap
45	Tuning slide return crook
46	Inside upper 3rd slide
47	Slide ferrule
48	Slide ferrule
49	Ballister brace - bell
50	Outside slide-lower
51	Outside slide - lower
52	Brace - val/tuning slide
53	Spring barrel - extension
A	Piston assembly
B	1st slide assembly
C	Tuning slide assembly
D	2nd slide assembly
E	3rd slide assembly

Key to Figure 8.36

102

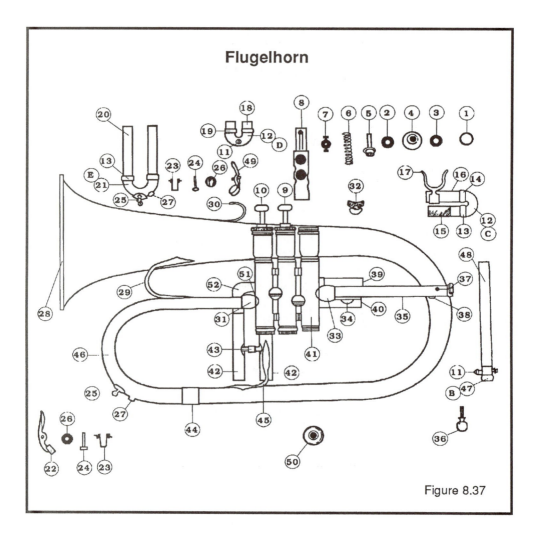

Flugelhorn

Figure 8.37

Flugelhorn — Key to Parts

ITEM NO.	NOMENCLATURE	ITEM NO.	NOMENCLATURE
1	Finger button	26	Water key cork
2	Piston stem felt	27	Water key nipple
3	Felt - black/white	28	Flugelhorn bell
4	Top cap	29	Bell/branch brace
5	Piston stem	30	Finger hook
7	Piston guide	31	Branch/valve ferrule
8	#1 piston	32	Ballister brace
9	#2 piston	33	Valve/mouthpipe ferrule
10	#3 piston	34	1st/mouthpipe brace
11	Pull knob	35	Outside mouthpipe tube
12	Slide crook	36	Thumbscrew
13	Slide ferrule	37	Split nut
14	Slide ferrule	38	Bell/mouthpipe brace
15	Lower inside 1st slide	39	Inside upper 1st slide
16	Upper outside 1st slide	40	Outside lower 1st slide
17	Thumbthrow	41	Valve assembly
18	Inside 2nd slide	42	Outside 3rd slide
19	2nd slide ferrule	43	3rd slide brace assembly
20	3rd slide inside slide	44	Bell/branch ferrule
21	Slide crook	45	Branch/3rd slide brace
22	Water key lever	46	Flugelhorn branch
23	Water key spring	47	Mouthpiece receiver
24	Water key screw	48	Mouthpipe tube
25	Water key bridge	49	3rd valve water key asseml
		50	Bottom valve cap

Key to Figure 8.37

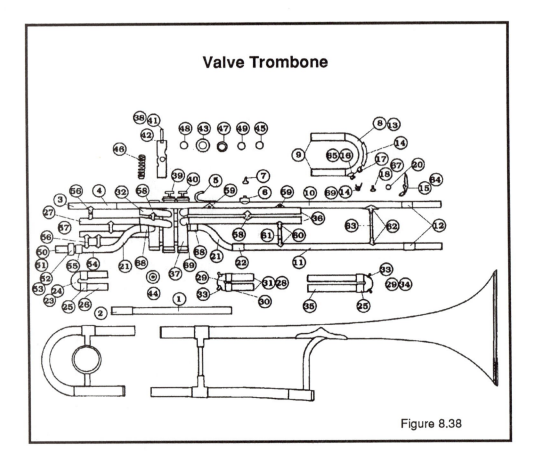

Valve Trombone

Figure 8.38

Valve Trombone — Key to Parts

ITEM NO.	NOMENCLATURE	ITEM NO.	NOMENCLATURE
1	Venturi	35	Inside slide tubes
2	Mouthpiece receiver	36	Outside slide tubes
3	Mouthpiece ferrule (old style not shown)	37	Valve case assembly
4	Sleeve	38	#1 piston with stem & guide
5	Finger hook	39	#2 piston with stem & guide
6	Lyre holder	40	#3 piston with stem & guide
7	Lyre screw	41	Piston stem
8	Tuning slide assembly	42	Piston guide
9	Outside slide tube	43	Top vale cap
10	Upper inside tube, 27-11/32"	44	Bottom valve cap
11	Lower inside tube, 15-1/16"	45	Finger button
12	Ferrule	46	Piston springs
13	Crook	47	Felt washer for top cap
14	Guard plate	48	Felt washer, piston stem
15	Water key (old style)	49	Felt washer, finger button
16	Water key bridge (old style)	50	Slide receiver tapered 2165
17	Water key nipple	51	Slide receiver tapered 2166
18	Water key screw (old style)	52	Bell lock nut 2165
19	Water key spring (old style)	53	Bell lock nut 2166
20	Water key cork	54	Sleeve
21	Gooseneck, leads to 1st & 3rd casing	55	Ferrule for gooseneck
22	Ferrule for gooseneck	56	Receiver to 1st slide
23	First valve slide assembly	57	#1 slide brace
24	Crook	58	#2 slide brace
25	Ferrule	59	Mouthpipe to #3 slide brace
26	Inside slide tube	60	#3 slide to lower long tube sockets
27	Outside slide tube	61	#3 slide to lower long tube rods
28	Second valve slide assembly	62	Main slide brace sockets
29	Crook	63	Main slide brace rod
30	Ferrule	64	Water key (new style)
31	Inside slide tube	65	Water key bridge (new style)
32	Outside tube	66	Water key spring (new style)
33	Pull knob	67	Water key screw (new style)
34	Third valve slide assembly	68	Ferrule
		69	#3 valve crooks

Key to Figure 8.38

106

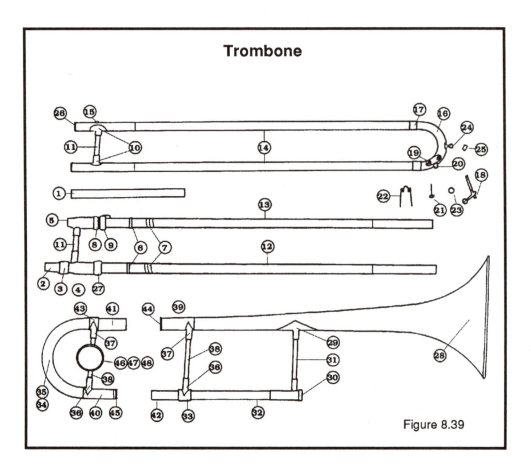

Trombone

Figure 8.39

Trombone — Key to Parts

ITEM
NO.   NOMENCLATURE

SLIDE ASSEMBLY

1	Mouthpipe, venturi tube
2	Tapered slide receiver
3	Slide receiver lock nut
4	Cork receiver, bell side
5	Cork receiver with slide lock, mouthpipe side
6	Cork washer
7	Cork receiver springs
8	Slide lock threaded retainer, male
9	Slide lock rings with hook, female
10	Brace sockets, hand slide
11	Brace tubes, hand slide
12	Inside slide tube, bell side, long
13	Inside slide tube, mouthpiece side, short
14	Outside slide tubes
15	Slide lock lug
16	Crook, hand slide
17	Ferrules
18	Water key
19	Water key bridge
20	Water key nipple
21	Water key pin
22	Water key spring
23	Water key cork
24	Guard plate with post
25	Rubber bumper tips
26	Sleeve ring
27	Cork receiver ferrule

BELL ASSEMBLY

28	Bell
29	Bell brace socket, large
30	Bell receiver
31	Brace tube
32	Gooseneck
33	Ferrule, small
34	Main tuning slide
35	Crook
36	Brace socket, small side (2)
37	Brace socket, large side (2)
38	Brace tubes (2)
39	Outside slide tube, large
40	Outside slide tube, small
41	Inside slide tube, large
42	Inside slide tube, small
43	Ferrule, large
44	Bead ring, large
45	Bead ring, small
46	Balancer (2 pcs.)
47	Balancer screws (2)
48	Emblem, balancer (2)

Key to Figure 8.39

Marching French Horn

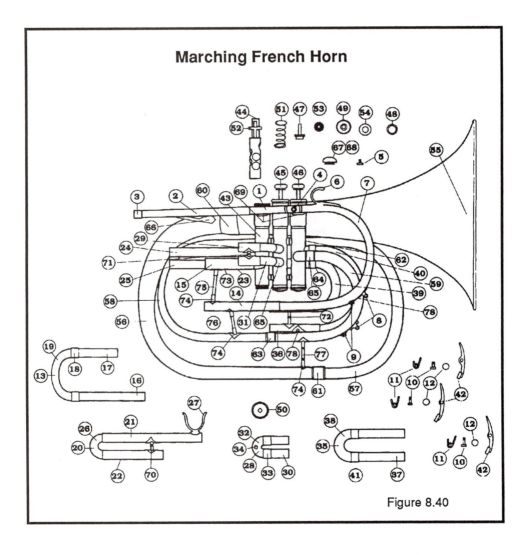

Figure 8.40

Marching French Horn — Key to parts

ITEM NO.	NOMENCLATURE	ITEM NO.	NOMENCLATURE
1	Mouthpipe assembly	39	Crook - medium
2	Mouthpipe sleeve	40	Crook - large
3	Mouthpiece receiver	41	Ferrules
4	Lyre holder	42	Water key - for #3 slide and #3 branch
5	Lyre screw		mouthpipe
6	Finger hook	43	Casing assembly
7	Mouthpipe tube	44	#1 valve piston
8	Water key bridge	45	#2 valve piston
9	Water key nipple	46	#3 valve piston
10	Water key screw	47	Piston stem
11	Water key spring	48	Finger button
12	Water key cork (hd)	49	Top valve cap
13	Main tuning slide assembly	50	Bottom valve cap
14	Outside slide tube, long	51	Piston spring
15	Outside slide tube, short	52	Piston guide
16	Inside slide tube, long	53	Piston felt (per hd)
17	Inside slide tube, short	54	Top cap washer (neoprene)
18	Ferrules	55	Bell, engraved
19	Crook	56	Bell bow branch
20	First valve slide assembly	57	#1 branch
21	Outside slide tube, upper	58	#2 branch
22	Outside slide tube, lower	59	#3 branch
23	Outside slide tube - short 2-1/4"	60	Bell connecting ring
24	Inside slide tube - long	61	Bow to branch ring
25	Inside slide tube - short	62	#1 to #2 branch ring
26	Crook	63	#2 to #3 branch ring
27	Thumb saddle	64	#3 to valve casing ferrule
28	Second valve slide assembly	65	Ferrule
29	Outside slide tubes	66	Bell to mouthpipe
30	Inside slide tubes	67	#1 valve casing to bell
31	Outside tubes curved (Connector crooks)	68	#3 valve casing to bell
32	Crook	69	Valve casing leadpipe (2)
33	Ferrules	70	#1 slide
34	Pull knob	71	#2 slide
35	Third valve slide assembly	72	#3 slide
36	Outside slide tube	73	#1 slide to main tuning slide
37	Inside slide tube	74	Brace socket
38	Crook - small	75	Main slide rod (1)
		76	#2 branch to main slide rod (1)
		77	Brace rod - #3 branch to bow branch
		78	#2 branch to #3 slide

Key to Figure 8.40

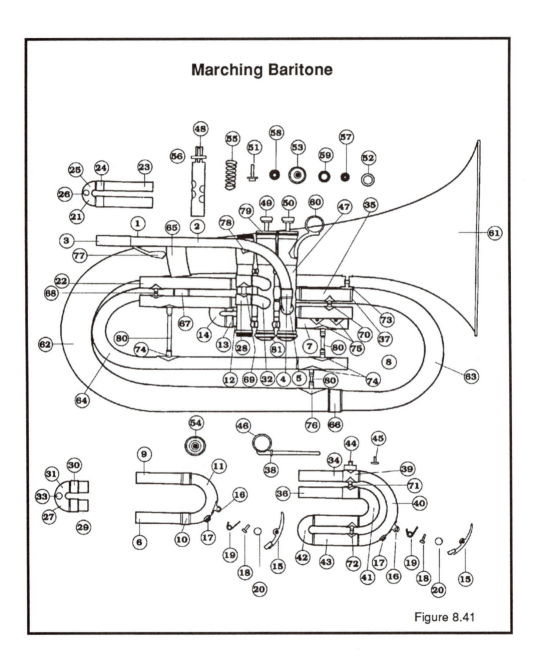

Marching Baritone

Figure 8.41

Marching Baritone — Key to Parts

ITEM NO.	NOMENCLATURE	ITEM NO.	NOMENCLATURE
1	Mouthpipe assembly	42	Crook - small 180°
2	Mouthpipe tube	43	Outside slide tubes 2-3/8" lower
3	Mouthpiece receiver	44	Lyre holder
4	Ferrule	45	Lyre screw
5	Knuckle crook (leads to #3 valve casing)	46	Finger ring
		47	Casing assembly
6	Main tuning slide assembly	48	#1 valve piston
7	Outside slide tube - valve side	49	#2 valve piston
8	Outside slide tube	50	#3 valve piston
9	Inside slide tubes	51	Piston stem
10	Ferrules	52	Finger button
11	Crook	53	Top valve cap
12	Extension tube	54	Bottom valve cap
13	Ferrules (lead to small 180° crook)	55	Piston springs
14	Crook 180° small	56	Piston guide
15	Water key	57	Felt washer for finger button
16	Water key bridge	58	Felt washer for piston stem
17	Water key nipple	59	Felt washer for top valve cap
18	Water key screw	60	Finger ring (soldered to 3rd casing)
19	Water key spring	61	Bell, engraved
20	Water key cork	62	#1 branch
21	First valve slide assembly	63	#2 branch
22	Outside slide tubes	64	#3 branch
23	Inside slide tubes	65	Bell connecting ring
24	Ferrules	66	Ring #1 to #2 branch
25	Crook	67	Ring #2 to #3 branch
26	Slide pull knob	68	#1 slide brace
27	Second valve slide assembly	69	#2 slide brace
28	Outside slide tubes	70	#3 slide brace (between stationary tubes)
29	Inside slide tubes		
30	Ferrules	71	#3 slide brace (between ferrules)
31	Crook	72	#3 slide brace (between lower slide tubes)
32	Knuckle crooks		
33	Slide pull knob	73	Bell to #2 branch brace
34	Third valve slide assembly	74	Main tuning slide brace sockets
35	Outside slide tubes (lead to valve casing)	75	Main slide to #3 slide
		76	Brace socket #1 branch
36	Inside slide tubes	77	Brace receiver to bell
37	Stop ring	78	Brace mouthpipe to #1 valve casing
38	Nylon stop ring	79	Brace bell to #2 valve casing
39	Ferrules	80	Brace rods available for above brace socket 3/16" diameter, 2-5/8" long
40	Crook - large 180°		
41	Crook - medium 180°	81	Cross brace, #2 valve

Key to Figure 8.41

Sousaphone

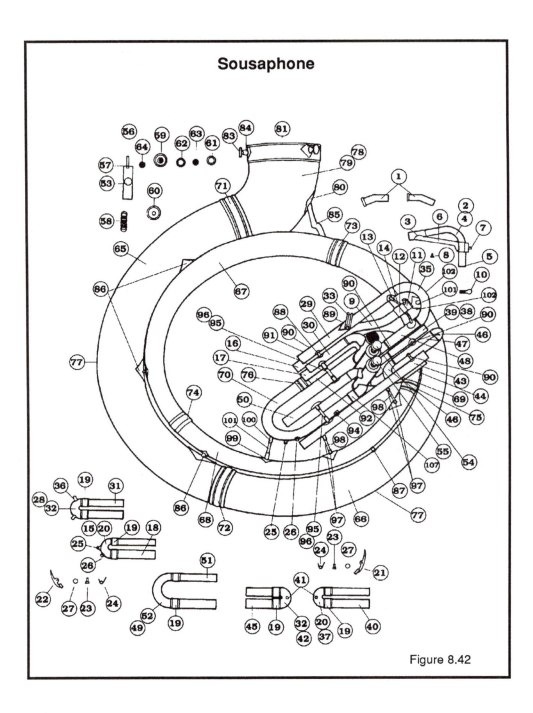

Figure 8.42

Sousaphone — Key to Parts

ITEM NO.	NOMENCLATURE	ITEM NO.	NOMENCLATURE
1	Tuning bits, BRIGHT SILVER PLATE, per pair	54	#2 piston with stem and guide
	Tuning bits, LACQUER, per pair	55	#3 piston with stem and guide
	Tuning bits, SATIN SILVER, per pair	56	Piston stem
2	Complete mouthpipe w/lyre holder and screw, LACQUER	57	Piston guide
	Complete mouthpipe w/lyre holder and screw, SATIN SILVER	58	Piston springs
		59	Top valve cap
	Complete mouthpipe w/lyre holder and screw, BRIGHT SILVER PLATE	60	Bottom valve cap
3	Receiver, part tuning bit fits into	61	Finger button
4	Mouthpipe bent tube	62	Top cap felt washer
5	Mouthpipe slide, part fitting into gooseneck	63	Finger button washer
		64	Piston stem washer
6	Mouthpipe brace	65	#1 branch with guard wire and ring for 2350
7	Lyre holder	66	#2 branch for 2350
8	Lyre screw	67	#3 branch for 2350
9	Gooseneck	68	#4 branch for 2350
10	Mouthpipe tightening screw	69	#5 branch
11	Mouthpipe receiver on gooseneck	70	#6 branch
12	Gooseneck brace ferrule assembly	71	Bow to #1 branch ring
13	Gooseneck brace socket assembly	72	#2 to #1 branch ring
14	Gooseneck brace rod	73	#3 to #2 branch ring
15	Main tuning slide assembly	74	#3 to #4 branch ring
16	Outside slide tube, long	75	4th to 5th branch ring
17	Outside slide tube, short	76	5th to 6th branch ring
18	Inside slide tube	77	Guard wire (35" only)
19	Ferrule	78	Bow assembly
20	Crook	79	Bow
21	Water key for 6th branch	80	Bow cap
22	Water key only	81	Bow mounting ring
23	Water key screw	82	Bell mounting ring
24	Water key spring	83	Bell screw
25	Water key bridge	84	Bell screw flange
26	Water key nipple	85	#3 branch to body bow brace
27	Water key cork	86	#1 branch to #3 branch braces
28	First valve slide assembly	87	#2 branch to #4 branch brace
29	Outside slide tube, long	88	1st slide brace
30	Outside slide tube, short, 4"	89	Gooseneck to 1st slide brace
31	Inside slide tube	90	Brace
32	Crook, small	91	Main tuning slide brace to 1st slide brace
33	Thumb ring	92	Main tuning slide to 5th branch brace
34	Outside slide tube, 3-3/8"	93	1st to 2nd slide brace
35	Crook, large	94	Lower 3rd slide to 6th branch brace
36	Pull knob	95	3rd slide brace socket
37	Second valve slide assembly	96	3rd slide brace rod
38	Outside slide tube, long	97	3rd slide to 4th branch socket
39	Outside slide tube, short	98	3rd slide to 4th branch rod
40	Inside slide tubes	99	6th to 4th brace socket, large
41	Pull knob	100	6th to 4th brace socket, small
42	Upper third valve slide assembly	101	Rod
43	Outside slide tube, long	102	#2 branch to 1st slide socket, large
44	Outside slide tube, short	103	#2 branch to 1st slide socket, small
45	Inside slide tube		
46	Crook		
47	Outside slide tube upper		
48	Outside slide tube lower		
49	Lower third valve slide assembly		
50	Outside slide tube, short		
51	Inside slide tube		
52	Crook		
53	#1 piston with stem and guide		

Key to Figure 8.42

BIBLIOGRAPHY

BRASS INSTRUMENTS

Bach, V. *Selmer Bandwagon*. Elkhart, Indiana: Selmer, 1967.

———. *Embouchure and Mouthpiece Manual*. Elkhart, Indiana: Vincent Bach, 1968.

———. *Bach Brass*, Elkhart, Indiana: Selmer, 1986.

Bains, A. *Brass Instruments, Their History and Development*. New York, New York: Scribner, 1976.

Deming, H. "Trumpet/Cornet Intonation Problems." *Brass Anthology*, Volume III. Northfield, Illinois: The Instrumentalist Company, 1986. (Article written in 1959.)

Donington, R. *Music and Its Instruments*. New York, New York: Methuen, 1982.

Evans, T. "Materials for Mouthpieces." *Brass Anthology*, Volume III. Northfield, Illinois: The Instrumentalist Company, 1986. (Article written in 1952.)

Forsythe, C. *Orchestration*. New York, New York: Macmillan, 1949.

Getchell, R. *Teacher's Guide to the Brass Instruments*. Elkhart, Indiana: Selmer, 1959.

Hail, J. "The Rotary Valve Trumpet : An American Revival." *Brass Anthology*, Volume III. Northfield, Illinois: The Instrumentalist Company, 1986. (Article written in 1972.)

Malek, V. "Tone Production." *Brass Anthology*, Volume III. Northfield, Illinois: The Instrumentalist Company, 1986. (Article written in 1954.)

Menke, W. *History of the Trumpet of Bach and Handel*. London, UK: Reeves, 1934.

Mueller, K. *Complete Guide to the Maintenance and Repair of Band Instruments*. New York, New York: Parker, 1982.

Olson, R. "Brass Instrument Bore." *Brass Anthology*, Volume

III. Northfield, Illinois: The Instrumentalist Company, 1986. (Article written in 1963.)

Schilke, R. "Dimensional Characteristics of Brass Mouthpieces." *Brass Anthology*, Volume III. Northfield, Illinois: The Instrumentalist Company, 1986. (Article written in 1952.)

————. "How to Select a Brass Mouthpiece." *Brass Anthology*, Volume III. Northfield, Illinois: The Instrumentalist Company, 1986. (Article written in 1966.)

————. "Practical Physics for Trumpeters and Teachers." *Brass Anthology*, Volume III. Northfield, Illinois: The Instrumentalist Company, 1986. (Article written in 1977.)

Tiede, C. *Practical Band Instrument Repair Manual*. Dubuque, Iowa: William C. Brown, 1970.

Werden. "Euphonium Mouthpieces: A Teachers' Guide." *Brass Anthology*, Volume III. Northfield, Illinois: The Instrumentalist Company, 1986. (Article written in 1981.)

CHAPTER NINE

NON-FRETTED STRING INSTRUMENTS

The general principles of acoustics, design, and construction of non-fretted string instruments are very similar. These instruments also share most of their characteristic design and sound production processes. Unlike the vast variety of brass instruments created through the centuries, non-fretted string instruments have only four different members in their family. Yet, while three of them might almost be considered graduated enlargements of the violin, there are some significant differences among them that need explaining.

THE VIOLIN

The violin is unique among instruments. A study of the design, construction, and workings of the violin will reveal the most magnificent enigma in musical instrument technology. The instrument is essentially a shapely hollow box about fourteen inches long and eight inches across at its widest point. It is fitted with a neck, a fingerboard, pegs, a tailpiece, an end button, a bridge, and strings (fig. 9.1).

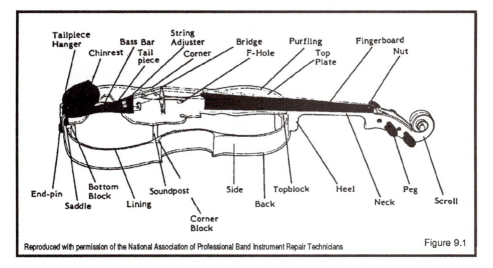

Reproduced with permission of the National Association of Professional Band Instrument Repair Technicians

Figure 9.1

The principles of acoustics that apply to the violin have been investigated by the greatest minds in history. Although significant progress has been made in understanding and documenting the manner in which the violin produces and amplifies sound, there are still forces within the design of the instrument which defy logical explanation. Manufacturers still do not know how to reproduce a Stradivarius-quality instrument. It appears that there is still more to comprehending the workings of the instrument than is implied by its simple appearance. The violin is constructed of 70 parts, has a range of four octaves and in the hands of a virtuoso, is the most versatile instrument in the orchestra. Its capacity to produce music is limited only by that of its maker and player.

SOUND GENERATION

Non-fretted string instruments can generate sound in several ways. The method most often used is drawing a horsehair *bow* across the string. To achieve a different effect, the strings can be *plucked* by the player's fingers. Other possible methods of generating vibrations on a string are not as common but still deserve mention. They are: activation by *sympathetic vibration*, i.e., motion caused by another sound source; drawing the *wooden stick* or back of the bow across the string; or bouncing the stick of the bow on the string in a succession of rapid strikes. The use of the wood of the bow, either drawn or bounced, is a special effect, whereas the sympathetic vibration may be classified as an acoustical phenomenon. The vibrating string, however activated, is the sound generator for non-fretted string instruments. When the string is set into motion, it emits a sound that is transferred to the body or amplifier of the instrument via the bridge.

BOW

The *bow* is the primary tool used to generate sound on a non-fretted string instrument. As such, it is given a great deal of consideration when a string player is selecting equipment. As the bow evolved, it was determined that *pernambuco wood*, primarily grown in Brazil, was the most satisfactory wood for the stick, since that wood is most resilient and at the same time very strong.

A number of other materials are presently used in the manufacturing of bow sticks, but with varying degrees of effectiveness. These include Brazil wood, pear wood, plastic, fiberglass, and light metals such as aluminum. All of these products are functional, yet each has its shortcomings. Pernambuco remains the most effective material for string instrument bow sticks.

Figure 9.2 illustrates how the stick of a bow is strung with

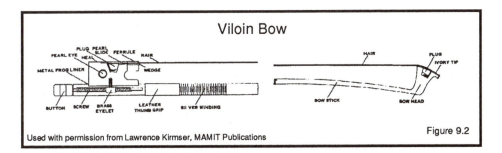

Viloin Bow

Used with permission from Lawrence Kirmser, MAMIT Publications

Figure 9.2

horsehair. A hank of hair is selected and combed so that all hairs are parallel to each other. The end of the hank is then tied and wedged securely into a box-shaped cutout (mortise) at the tip of the bow. The hair is held in place by a wooden, wedge-shaped plug that is accurately cut to exactly fit the space remaining in the cutout box. This plug holds the hair in place. A ferrule is inserted over the hair which is carefully drawn along the bow and inserted into a similar box-shaped cutout in the frog. Again a wooden wedge is placed into the box to secure the hair in place. Finally, a slide and another wooden wedge are inserted between the ferrule and the frog to help distribute the hairs equally and laterally and to keep them in place.

When viewed with the naked eye, horsehair appears to be smooth, but under examination with a microscope, the surface of the hair is quite rough. Particles, called follicles, project from the hair, forming an abrasive surface. The application of rosin, a substance produced from tree sap derivatives, to the abrasive surface produces a gripping character in the hair. When the bow hair is drawn across a string on an instrument, the hair grips the string and excites it into motion causing the vibration that produces a tone. The quality of that tone depends greatly on the quality of the bow hair and the expertise with which that hair was installed on the bow.

If a string is plucked, it will begin to vibrate. When touched with a finger, the vibration will stop. One might then wonder why a string will vibrate when a bow is in continuous contact with that string and yet stop vibrating when it is touched by another object. The answer is that the bow is not really in continuous contact with the string. The bow is instead gripping and releasing the string in a rapid sequence which replicates a plucking action. This action causes the string to be drawn to a point where its lateral tension is sufficient to overcome the gripping force of the rosined bow hair (fig. 9.3). At that

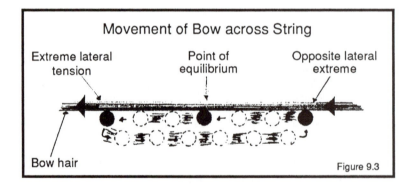

Figure 9.3

time the string releases itself from the bow and returns to cross its point of equilibrium, proceeds to its opposite lateral extreme, only to be gripped again by the bow hair and then to repeat the process. All of this occurs in such rapid succession that it is invisible to the naked eye. The final effect is one of a string being gripped by the bow hair, pulled to a point of tension, breaking free from that grip, rebounding to a point opposite the point from which it was just released and then being caught again by the bow hair, only to repeat the process.

STRINGS

A number of different materials are currently being used for the manufacture of strings. Among the most common are gut, steel, perlon (a type of plastic fiber), silk, chromium/steel, and gold. With the exception of the gold strings, all of the other products can be used as a core for strings that are then wound with aluminum, chromium, or silver. This process can be used for all strings except the violin 'E' string which, due to its high pitch, does not require the acoustical enhancement provided by wrapping.

Each type of string construction produces a different quality of sound and can alter the overall tone quality of an instrument. The choice of strings, therefore, becomes a matter worthy of great consideration. One may elect to brighten or darken the tone quality of an instrument by selecting the string material that creates the desired effect. When striving to achieve a particular tone, one must consider the individual timbre of each string instrument in conjunction with how that instrument will respond to each type of string. Unfortunately there are no prescriptions for making this determination, and so, one must rely on experimentation to arrive at the combination of string and instrument that will satisfy the individual taste of the performer.

Although there are no concrete rules for selecting strings that will produce a particular sound, the following are some general guidelines which may facilitate the choice.

Steel strings are most durable, produce the most aggressive or brightest sound, stay in tune longer and are generally prescribed for use by beginning players.

Gut strings usually produce a more mellow sound, but since they react to changes in temperature and humidity, they tend to break more easily and are most susceptible to intonation problems.

Gut core strings, which are *wound with silver* or *aluminum,* retain the characteristics of the pure gut except that they tend to have a fuller sound and somewhat greater durability.

Perlon, a plastic substance, is used as a core for wound strings. It is stronger than gut, does not react greatly to temperature and humidity changes, and tends to stay in tune longer. Perlon strings produce a slightly more aggressive sound than gut strings.

AMPLIFICATION

The sound that a string emits when it is bowed or plucked is weak at best and would make little contribution to a musical performance. It is the amplification of that sound that transforms it from an insignificant whimper to a valuable musical tone. The quality of the tone is almost entirely dependent on the proficiency of the performer in conjunction with the quality and adjustment of the instrument being played. When produced by a proficient performer and amplified by a good instrument, the sound is transformed into a desirable tone that produces music. It is important to note that the operative terms here are *proficient performer* and *good instrument*, for weakness on the part of either will negate the effectiveness of the other.

BRIDGE

When a bow is properly drawn across a string, the sound that is generated is conducted to the top or belly of the instrument by a *bridge*. (fig. 9.4). As the string is set into vibration, its transversal

Bridge for Members of the Violin Family

Figure 9.4

(side to side) motion is converted by the bridge into a perpendicular (up and down) 'stamping' motion. The feet of the bridge transfer the vibrations by actually stamping on the belly of the instrument. Since the bridge plays a dominant role in transferring the sound from the string to the amplifier (body) of the instrument, the design and material used to construct the bridge and its placement on the instrument must be calculated to fill that function in the best possible way.

Simply stated, the dimensions for non-fretted string instrument bridges are unique to each instrument. Although there are some guidelines for the initial cutting of the bridge, the final product must be cut to fit the contour of the top of the instrument and to provide sufficient, but not excessive height for the strings to clear the fingerboard. Serious consideration must also be given to the spacing of the strings on the bridge so that they will span evenly over the fingerboard, starting from the nut and extending to the bridge.

Figure 9.5 is a chart of recommended dimensions for the four instruments of the violin family.

INSTRUMENT	HEIGHT*	THICKNESS (TOP)	STRING SPACING
VIOLIN	E 1/8" G 3/16"	1/16"	7/16"
VIOLA	A 3/16" C 1/4"	1/16"	1/2"
CELLO	A 1/4" C 5/16"	3/32"	5/8"
BASS	G 7/16" E 11/16"	3/16"	1-1/8"

*Note that the height of a bridge is measured as the distance it elevates the strings above the end of the fingerboard at two points: the highest and lowest pitched strings. The two intermediate strings are set proportionately following the contour of the end of the fingerboard. If the strings are properly set, the player will be able to bow each string comfortably without inadvertently bowing two strings simultaneously.

Figure 9.5

The most common material used for bridge construction is hard maple. It is essential that the wood be hard, for it must withstand the pressure and friction of the taut strings. Sometimes inserts of even harder material are used (especially at the point on the bridge where the violin 'E' string makes contact) in order to withstand the cutting action of that very thin, taut string. Ebony, cowhide, rubber or plastic are used in various ways to help prevent wear on the point of contact where the strings meet the bridge.

The placement of the bridge on the body of the instrument is crucial to obtaining optimum sound production. The feet of the bridge must be cut to fit the contour of the top of the instrument. The feet must then be spaced so that the left foot stands over the bass bar while the right foot stands slightly behind (toward the fingerboard side) the sound post (fig. 9.6). In this position the right foot of the bridge conducts the higher tones to the top of the instrument and on to the sound post, which then carries the sound to the back of the instrument. The left foot conducts the lower tones to the bass bar that transverses lengthwise along the instrument.

SOUND POST AND BASS BAR

The *sound post* and *bass bar* together distribute sound throughout the box or body, which acts as an amplifier for the sounds generated by the strings. The motion of the components of the body then stimulate the air pocket contained within the body into vibrating patterns of compression and rarefaction. This motion takes the form of a pumping force. It amplifies the sound generated at the string and transports it through the bridge, belly, sound post and bass bar to ultimately produce the tone of the instrument.

The function of the *bass bar* is twofold. It *reinforces* the top of the instrument supporting the great force exerted upon the top by the tension of the strings. It also *distributes the vibrations* laterally throughout the top. The interaction of the parts of the instrument 'pumps' the air within the body in and out through the 'f' holes, amplifying the initial sound generated by the bow/ string team.

The *sound post* plays an important role in sound transmission. In addition to acting as a

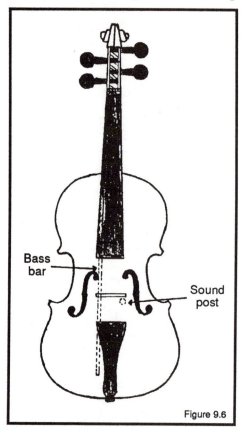

Bass bar

Sound post

Figure 9.6

structural support for the top of the instrument, this post, made of soft wood, conducts the vibrations from the top of the instrument to its back. The sound post distributes tones produced by the higher strings to the back of the instrument, while muting any echo effect which would occur if that post were not present.

SIDES AND BACK

The *sides* and *back* of the instrument are made of a harder wood, usually maple, and are thicker than the belly of the violin. The function of the sides and back, in addition to enhancing the vibrating process, is to form the supporting structure for the entire instrument. The tension incurred by the strings stretched from the top (pegs) to the bottom (tailpiece), some 68 lbs. (31 kg), draws the top (scroll end) and bottom of the instrument (tail piece end) toward each other. It is the strength of the back plate, with the aid of the sides, that prevents the belly (of a softer wood) from folding in half.

There are two parts of the sound amplifier that appear to be ornamental but play an important role in production of sound. These are the sound holes or *'f' holes* (so named because of their shape) and the purfling which appears to be an ornamental trim inlaid around the edge of the top and back of the body (fig. 9.7).

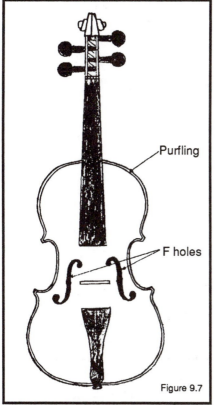

Purfling

F holes

Figure 9.7

F HOLES AND PURFLING

The *'f' holes* significantly affect the quality of the tone of the instrument. The flexing action of the mid-portion of the top of the instrument, and the ability of the tone-saturated air within the sound box to escape, are affected by the size, shape, and location of the holes. Due to the importance of these shapely orifices, their exact shape, size, and location are distinctive to each craftsman.

Purfling consists of two parallel strips of hard wood, usually ebony, which are inlaid into the surface around the edge of the top and back of the violin. The purfling serves an important acoustical purpose. Since the purfling is inlaid into the top and back of the instrument, the groove cut for the inlay acts as a barrier or interruption for the vibration that is traveling through the woods. As a result, the maker is able to define clearly the area throughout which the vibration is to take place and thereby control that vibrating area and the tone it produces.

In summary, the complete amplifying process on non-fretted string instruments is shown in figure 9.8. The string's vibrations (1) are conducted by the hardwood (usually maple) bridge (2) to the softer wood (usually spruce) top plate (3) of the instrument's body, are then transported *via* the softwood soundpost (4) to the hardwood back (5) of the instrument, and via the softwood bass bar (6) laterally throughout the entire top. The hardwood back and softer wood top (belly) are joined by hardwood sides (7). Combined, the top, sides, and back form an air space (8) in which the sound circulates. The interaction of all

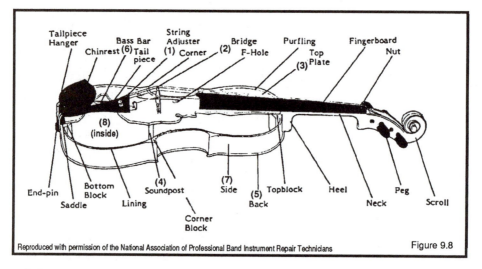

Reproduced with permission of the National Association of Professional Band Instrument Repair Technicians

Figure 9.8

of these components forms the amplifier for string instruments. In spite of the three-hundred-year history of the violin, the exact interaction which takes place among these components is not yet fully understood.

The mathematical simplicity and consistency of the design of the instrument becomes evident when one observes that violins hardly vary in their proportions. The greatest amount of wood is found beneath the bridge. The thickness of the wood decreases to half the amount at the sides of the instrument while remaining consistent throughout the length of the bass bar. Further across the top of the instrument the measurement at the thinnest part of the top becomes equal to one quarter of the thickest part. The *ratios* then progress from the *whole* (thickest) to *one-half* of the whole, (medium) to *one-quarter* (thinnest) of the whole.

The amplifier of a violin is deceptive in its simple appearance and yet it utilizes a most complex system for distributing vibrations. The vibrations are carried throughout the physical structure of the wooden body of the instrument and travel in every direction. This diversity of movement causes the instrument to vibrate and oscillate horizontally, vertically, and diagonally. Simultaneously, the air contained within the body is set into motion, increasing and decreasing in volume while traveling in and out of the body through the 'f' holes.

A study of the bodies or amplifiers of the woodwind and brass instruments determined that their main functions were first, to contain the columns of air that were set into motion, and second, to act as a structure into which various mechanical devices were incorporated to extend or shorten that vibrating air column. The quality of the tone was a product of the sound generator, i.e., the mouthpiece, reed, etc. In the case of the violin family, the body acts as the amplifier of sound as well as the portion of the instrument that profoundly affects the quality of tone produced. An expertly crafted violin strung with a given set of strings and played with an appropriate bow, will produce a better tone than a poorer quality instrument set up with the same bow and strings. Unlike wind instruments, the tone quality of string instruments is largely a product of the quality of the material used in the construction of the body of the instrument and of the design and craftmanship used in making that particular instrument.

MECHANISM

The *mechanics* of the violin and its design are models of simplicity compared to the manner in which these parts interact when set into motion. The previous sections have described the bow and strings as the sound generating mechanism; the bridge, sound post, and bass bar as sound conductors; and the body of the instrument as an amplifier. The remaining parts of the instrument are even simpler in concept and are almost static even when in motion. The violin's mechanisms are not complex sets of levers, screws, posts, pads and springs but rather simply shaped wooden wedges, plates and strips. They are designed and crafted to support the strings and permit the player to shorten the open strings in order to raise the pitches from the original tuning.

Figure 9.8 is a diagram of the violin showing the interior and exterior parts. The mechanism that supports the sound generating systems consists of the scroll, peg box, pegs, neck, fingerboard, bridge, saddle, tailpiece, tailgut, and end button. The body (amplifier) of the instrument is made up of a top (belly), 'f' holes, sides (ribs or bout), a back (back plate) and purfling surrounding the top and back plates. These parts form the exterior or visible portion of the body. Supporting the exterior of the instrument are the ribs, top and bottom block, corner blocks, bass bar and sound post.

The materials most commonly used for the construction of violins are spruce, maple, ebony and rosewood. The top of the violin is generally made of spruce since that is a softer wood and fills the design description for the most effective sound amplification. Spruce is also used for the sound post, linings, and the bass bar. The back, sides, gluing blocks, neck, and scroll are generally made of hard maple, again in compliance with the prescription for achieving the most responsive amplifier while maintaining structural integrity. Hard maple or a wood of similar strength is needed for these parts in order to support the tension exerted by the strings stretched across the instrument.

The *trim* on the instrument, (namely, the end button, saddle, tailpiece, fingerboard, nut, and pegs) is usually constructed of ebony, rosewood, or, in the case of low-quality instruments, less expensive hardwoods, metal, or plastic. All of the instruments of the violin family are constructed of the same materials and essentially use the same technology in practically the same manner. The only difference will be found in the size and proportions of the larger instruments. In the construction of less expensive larger instruments, laminated wood is used to cut costs while improving the structural integrity of the instrument.

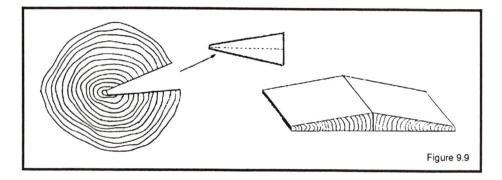

Figure 9.9

There are two ways in which wood can be cut for use in making the upper and lower plates (top and back) of the violin. If it is the intention of the maker to construct an instrument with a *two-piece back plate*, the wood would be cut into triangular shaped blocks which would then be cut vertically down the middle to form two triangles (fig. 9.9). These are then joined to form one plate that is subsequently carved into shape. This process is used in order to increase the likelihood of achieving a symmetrical wood grain pattern.

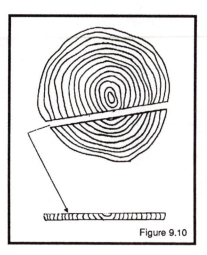

Figure 9.10

The second possibility is to cut a layer of wood that will produce a *one-piece plate*. This method removes the seam from the middle of the plate (fig. 9.10). The dis-advantage of this method is the likelihood that a *one piece slab* of wood, because of the span of the size required, will have a variation in grain as the cut progresses. It is most desirable to maintain a uniformity of grain in the production of these plates. The triangle cut maintains this uniformity because the cuts are taken from a smaller portion of the overall slab of wood.

THE FAMILY OF NON-FRETTED

STRING INSTRUMENTS

The family of non-fretted string instruments, often referred to as the *family of violins,* consists of the violin, viola, cello, and double bass. These instruments form a string choir that covers a range of about five-and-one-half octaves. Just as choral music uses the

The Family of Violins

Violin

Viola

Cello

Double Bass

Figure 9.11

soprano, alto, tenor, and bass voices, so the string choir uses the violin, viola, cello, and double bass (fig. 9.11).

The unique characteristic of the family of violins is that they are all constructed using the same design, acoustical principles, and manufacturing techniques. Instruments of the woodwind and brass choirs also have similarities within their respective groups, but they do not begin to approach the close relationship that the violin family shares: all four share the same process for initiating and amplifying sound.

Structural differences among these instruments, aside from their size and playing range, are slight. The violin, the most acoustically perfect of the four, was used as a model for a study of the entire family of non-fretted string instruments. The viola, cello and double bass are progressively (but not proportionately) larger while still maintaining essentially the same structure and design of the violin.

The *viola* is often described as being a large violin because both instruments share many characteristics of design, physics, construction, and appearance. The viola is tuned a fifth lower than the violin but is one-seventh larger. The difference in pitch is disproportionate to the difference in size, so the ratio of tuning to size results in the darker timbre associated with the viola.

One distinct difference between the two instruments is that while the body of a violin is almost always the same size, 14 inches (35.5 cm) long, the size of a viola body can vary as much as two inches. Another difference appears in the size-to-pitch ratio. An instrument which is tuned a perfect fifth below the violin should be considerably larger than the viola, if it were to follow the size-to-pitch ratio set by the design of the violin. In fact, the size of the viola should be so great that it would not be manageable as an instrument to be played under the chin. Since the size of the viola is not correctly proportioned to its tuning, viola makers can enjoy a bit of latitude when designing the instrument, and can alter the size to produce the tone quality desired.

The *cello*, or *violincello*, is also disproportionate in size to its difference in tuning. It is tuned a full octave below the viola but is smaller than its acoustical requirement. The discrepancy is compensated for by a significant increase in the depth or thickness of the body of the cello. With the increased depth, the lower tones are able to resonate with the characteristic timber of the cello.

Due to its relatively large size, the cello is supported by an *end pin* that extends from the bottom of the instrument (the point of the end button on the violin). The end pin is adjustable in order to accommodate different size players. The cello rests with its end pin on the floor, while the player balances the instrument between the knees. In this position, the strings are reversed from their positions on the violin and viola. The lowest string, the C string, now becomes the first string on the right hand of the player as opposed to violins and violas which have the highest string at the player's right side.

The *double bass* is the lowest-sounding instrument of the violin family. Although it too shares the principles of the string-instrument design explained above, the double bass has the greatest structural differences of the family. Double bass pegs are not wooden nor do they function on the wooden wedge principle. Due to the greater thickness of the strings, there is need for a stronger and more stable peg treatment. So evolved the *'worm and gear'* system now used exclusively on this instrument (fig. 9.12). This system is also used on fretted string instruments and can be installed on any of the other three instruments of the violin family. Such a modification is usually restricted to use on student instruments, since the worm and gear mechanism helps sustain the tuning of a string instrument. Unfortunately, this mechanism adds a considerable amount of weight to the peg box and so the advantages of easier tuning are outweighed by a possible problem of balance on the violin or viola. The use of the worm and gear system is more practical on the cello and the double bass, since the instrument rests on the floor and balance is less of a burden to the player.

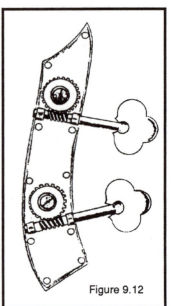

Figure 9.12

In addition to its larger size the double bass differs in appearance from the violin, viola, and cello. While the shoulders of these instruments are at a 90 degree angle from the fingerboard, the size of the double bass requires that the shoulders be sloped in order to allow the player to reach the higher fingering positions comfortably. Another difference is found in the back of the double bass. Rather than being rounded, the back of the larger instrument starts out from the heel of the neck sloping outward and then levels off to a flat back for the major portion of the instrument. This design allows the maker to use less than half of the wood required for a rounded back without sacrificing any structural integrity.

Some double basses are designed to have a fifth string, enabling the performer to play down to C'. An additional way to achieve this extended range is by installing a device that lowers the pitch of the fourth string to C'.

The violin, viola, cello and double bass, sharing most of the same technology, combine to make the most versatile choir of instruments in the contemporary music world. These instruments share their design, acoustical function, construction, and history. They enjoy a romantic quality that has resulted in their being considered collectibles, works of art, a three-century-old mystery story, and the heart of the modern symphony orchestra. Lest this writer be tempted to wax philosophical, he will end here.

SUMMARY

Sound is generated on a violin and all other non-fretted string instruments when a string is excited into vibration. The sound is conducted by the bridge to the top plate of the violin. The sound is then transferred to the back plate via the sound post and distributed laterally throughout the top plate by the bass bar. The combined motion of these parts sets the volume of air contained within the body into a pumping motion that forces the resonating sound out of the instrument through the 'f' holes. In this manner the violin produces sound.

BIBLIOGRAPHY

NON-FRETTED STRING INSTRUMENTS

Apel, W. *Harvard Dictionary of Music*. Cambridge, Massachusetts: Harvard University Press, 1961.

Bachmann, A. *An Encyclopedia of the Violin*. New York, New York: Da Capo, 1966.

Donington, R. *Music and Its Instruments*. New York, New York: Methuen, 1982.

Forsyth, C. *Orchestration*. New York, New York: Macmillan, 1949.

Gill, D. *The Book of the Violin*. New York, New York: Phaidon, 1984.

Herron-Allen. *Violin Making As It Was and Is*. London, UK: Ward Lock, 1985.

Liepp, E. *The Violin*. Toronto, Canada: University of Toronto Press, 1969.

Matesky, R. *String Teacher's Hand Book*. New York, New York: Alfred Music, 1970.

Mell, A. *Journal of The Violin Society of America*, Volume VII, No. 1. New York, New York: Queens College Press, 1984.

Paesold, R. *Catalogue of String Instruments*. New York, New York: Boosey and Hawkes, 1989.

Peterlongo, P. *The Violin, Its Physical and Acoustical Principles*. New York, New York: Taplinger, 1979.

Piston, W. *Orchestration*. New York, New York: W. W. Norton, 1955.

Randel, D. *The New Harvard Dictionary of Music*. Cambridge, Massachusetts: Harvard University Press, 1986.

Sadie, S. *The New Groves Dictionary of Musical Instruments*, Volumes I & III. New York, New York: Groves, 1984.

Scherl & Roth. *You Fix Them*. Cleveland, Ohio: Scherl and Roth, 1959.

Stewart, Adeau. *The Music Lover's Guide to the Instruments of the Orchestra*. New York, New York: Van Nostrand Reinhold, 1980.

Wechsberg, J. *The Glory of the Violin*. New York, New York: The Viking Press, 1973.